Stress, Tests, and Success

Stress, Tests, and Success

The Ultimate Law School Survival Guide

J. Keith Essmyer, Jr., Esq.

iUniverse, Inc.
New York Lincoln Shanghai

Stress, Tests, and Success
The Ultimate Law School Survival Guide

Copyright © 2005 by J. Keith Essmyer, Jr.

iUniverse books may be ordered through booksellers or by contacting:

iUniverse
2021 Pine Lake Road, Suite 100
Lincoln, NE 68512
www.iuniverse.com
1-800-Authors (1-800-288-4677)

ISBN: 0-595-34838-6

Printed in the United States of America

Dedicated to my parents, Dr. Joseph K. and Winnie A. Essmyer, in appreciation for the life long love of learning and education they instilled in me as a child.

Contents

Introduction

Why did I write this book? In August of 1997, I found myself heading to law school without a clue of what to expect when I got there. Having taken the Law School Admissions Test (LSAT) on a whim in February, while working on a Master's in English Literature at Southeast Missouri State University, I somehow managed to receive a high enough score to not feel too embarrassed about reporting it on a law school application. A few hastily prepared applications and an acceptance letter from the University of Missouri-Columbia's School of Law in hand, I found myself in late August loading up all of my possessions and moving to Columbia, Missouri, with my loving wife, Lisa, and my trusting pug dog, Sammy, by my side.

Being the first in my immediate family to attend law school and not knowing any lawyers personally, I quickly found myself wishing that I'd had a better idea of what to expect in law school and how to succeed once I got there. Unfortunately for me, this knowledge came too late and I found myself struggling through 3 years of one of the most demanding curriculums in American education without any idea of how to succeed. My struggles, however, mercifully ended in May of 2000, as I graduated with my Juris Doctorate (JD), much to the relief of my family and friends, and a class ranking securely fixed within the lower 50th percentile.

Having practiced law for sometime now, I have often found myself being asked by law students wanting to improve their future or current academic standing in law school for advice on how best to accomplish this not so simple goal. After quickly discovering that I could not possibly communicate in a single conversation all the secrets and tips I had learned the hard way during my torturous 3 years of law school, as well as all the insider knowledge that I have gained as a practicing attorney, I decided to write this book so that future and present law school students can avoid the academic pitfalls and failures that befell me in law school and be better prepared for making the transition from law student to new attorney.

As you will soon learn, this book is not like any other "How To Succeed In Law School" book out there. This book is a straightforward, no nonsense survival guide that is designed to be used and referenced by a law student throughout his or her law school career and during those nervous, beginning days of that first legal job. Unlike other law school success guides, this book is not 300+ pages in length but is designed to be read in a single one or two hour setting. Although this book is divided into three separate parts for first year law students, second year law students, and third year law students and new lawyers, I strongly recommend that you take the time to read through the entire book at least once, as much of the information contained in the book will be helpful to you no matter what stage of the law school experience you are in. Also, unlike other law school success guides, this book doesn't end at the final page but is designed to be added to as a student picks up his or her own secrets and survival tips on how to succeed in law school and as a new lawyer, which is why you will find several blank pages at the end of the book for notes. Students who take the time to read this book before starting law school and reference it during their 3 years in law school and during their days as a new attorney will find that they are better prepared than most students to succeed in law school and better prepared than most lawyers to succeed in the legal profession.

I provide no tips on achieving a high score on the LSAT and picking the right law school in this book because this book was designed for the law student who has already taken the LSAT, chosen a law school, and is heading to that law school with a desire to succeed. This book is designed to serve as the law student's survival guide from the first day of class, through graduation and the bar exam, and during that first legal job. Success is waiting for you law student. Now go and get it!

SIDEBAR: Sometimes in court the judge will want to discuss matters with the attorneys without the jury being able to hear their conversation. In these instances, the judge will call the attorneys to one side of the judge's bench to hold the discussion; such discussions are called sidebar conferences. Occasionally, I will call a sidebar to offer additional insights or tips on a subject. Your presence at these sidebars is strongly encouraged and respectfully requested.

SIDEBAR: Although I said I would not offer any tips on achieving a good LSAT score or choosing a law school, my conscious has gotten the better of me and I find that I must offer a few words of advice for anyone reading this book who has yet to take the LSAT or choose a law school. With regard to the LSAT, it is a test that a person should take the time to study and prepare for. There are a number of good LSAT study guides and preparation courses on the market today and I recommend that anyone planning to take the LSAT take full advantage of such guides and courses because the LSAT is graded in such a manner that you will want to achieve the best score you can on the test the first time you take it. More information on the LSAT can be found at the Law School Admission Council's website at www.lsac.org. As for choosing a law school, like the LSAT there are a number of good guides on the market today that can help you choose a law school. Also, *U.S. News and World Reports* annually publishes an issue ranking law schools throughout the country, as well as publishes annual guides to the best colleges and graduate schools. More information about *U.S. News and World Reports* and their college and graduate school rankings and guides can be found at www.usnews.com. My simple advice about choosing a law school is that if you are not one of those students who will be attending an Ivy League law school and you don't having a burning desire or need to attend a particular law school, choose the most affordable, accredited law school you can find because there is no need to pay Ivy League prices for a law degree you can get at state school prices. Remember, all the money that you or your parents borrow for law school has to be paid back someday.

PART I: 1L'S

SURVIVAL TIPS FOR THE FIRST YEAR LAW STUDENT

THE BEST SURVIVAL TIP I EVER GOT AS A LAW STUDENT

To prove to all you doubters out there that this book is different from any other "How To Succeed In Law School" book on the market today, I have decided to start with the best survival tip a law student could ever get, namely, BAR/BRI®. Remember this name, if it is the only thing you get out of this book you will be well ahead of most of your fellow law students. BAR/BRI is a company that specializes in producing bar review programs and materials for law students. Every summer, thousands of law school graduates crowd into lecture halls and classrooms across America to prepare for upcoming bar exams. Most of these graduates will be studying BAR/BRI materials, often times in a review program run by BAR/BRI personnel. Although BAR/BRI materials are often thought of in terms of bar review classes and programs, BAR/BRI outlines are some of the best outlines a law student could ever study while in law school because the outlines are easy to understand and contain a tremendous amount of detail about the subjects they cover. In other words, if you really want to understand what your law professors are talking about, get your hands on some BAR/BRI outlines.

BAR/BRI bar review outlines typically come in a two-volume set, with one volume covering the six subjects, Constitutional Law, Torts, Criminal Law/ Procedure, Evidence, Real Property, and Contracts, that are found on the Multistate portion of virtually every state's bar exam and are often mandatory classes for all law students in their first year. The other volume covers the subjects that are found on the essay portion of a state's bar exam, in Missouri these subjects include Administrative Law, Agency and Partnership, Commercial Paper, Conflicts of Law, Corporations and Limited Liability Companies, Equity (Remedies), Family Law, Federal Civil Procedure, Missouri Civil Procedure, Sales, Secured Transactions, Trusts and Future Interests, and Wills. As one can see, BAR/BRI outlines cover every subject on a state's bar exam and, if they can help a law school graduate better understand a subject for a bar exam, just think how helpful BAR/BRI outlines can be to a law school student. Consequently, law students should do what they can to get their hands on BAR/BRI outlines before they find themselves sitting in a law school classroom.

Although I receive no money for touting the virtues of BAR/BRI outlines, the material found in BAR/BRI outlines is so superior to any other commercial outline on the market today that I freely promote BAR/BRI outlines and encourage law students to seek them out. I can only imagine how different my law school experience might have been had someone whispered BAR/BRI in my ear on my first day as a law student. Additional information about the BAR/BRI company can be found at <u>www.barbri.com</u>.

SIDEBAR: BAR/BRI outlines are so good that many attorneys do not want to part with them after taking the bar exam and instead keep them in their offices as reference resources. Consequently, it may be hard to find BAR/BRI outlines without having to sign up and pay for a bar review course, which is somewhat expensive and is something a first year law student shouldn't be worried about. If you know a lawyer or have one in the family, you might start by asking them if they still have their BAR/BRI outlines and, if so, are they willing to part with the material while you are in law school. This is especially encouraged if the lawyer practices in the same state you are going to law school in or the state you are planning to take the bar exam in. Student book stores, in particular your law school bookstore, are good places to look for used BAR/BRI outlines. Online outlets and websites, such as Amazon.com and Ebay, are also good places to look for used BAR/BRI outlines. BAR/BRI outlines come in a large two-volume set and look like oversized, blue telephone books. BAR/BRI also has an abbreviated version of these outlines in a book, also blue but only one-volume, which is called the *Conviser Mini Review*; it is also a good study aide for law students. I encourage you to visit the BAR/BRI website to get an idea of what you are looking for before you buy any used BAR/BRI outlines. The more recent the BAR/BRI outline the better as, like most things, the law often changes with the passing of time.

SIDEBAR: Many law schools have an agreement with BAR/BRI to provide bar review materials for their graduating students. If you are having trouble locating some BAR/BRI outlines, you might try approaching your law school and asking if the school can help you obtain the outlines. Also, as you will see if you take the time to visit the BAR/BRI website, BAR/BRI offers additional study aides designed for law students presently in law school but, as I am unfamiliar with these materials, I cannot offer you an opinion on their quality or effectiveness.

SIDEBAR: Although BAR/BRI is the most recognized name in bar review material, it isn't the only name in the bar review market. If you find yourself having trouble finding BAR/BRI materials, visit your campus and local bookstores or search online for alternatives but remember that you are looking for bar review material that is used (i.e. discounted), as well as easy to read and easy to comprehend.

SIDEBAR: Now for some legal stuff, BAR/BRI is a registered trademark of the BAR/BRI Group, and all information contained in BAR/BRI materials are copyrighted by the BAR/BRI Group and its licensees, and may not be reproduced without the permission of the BAR/BRI Group.

BEFORE STARTING LAW SCHOOL

Before you even step foot on the college or university campus that is home to your chosen law school, you should have yourself mentally prepared for law school. In other words, get your priorities in order. Aside from your family, law school should be your number one priority. If you want to succeed in law school, you have to treat law school like a **50–70 hours per week job**. Your job for the next 3 years is to go to law school and succeed, nothing more nothing less. The sooner you start approaching law school like a job, a very demanding job that requires the highest degree of professionalism, the sooner you will be outperforming your classmates who just see law school as another course of study like their undergraduate studies were. Law school is not the cakewalk that many law students found their undergraduate studies to be. Law school is a very demanding endeavor that every law student needs to prepare him or herself for mentally.

> **SIDEBAR:** When law school starts so does your job of being a law student. Show up early and be prepared to stay late. Even when you are tired, you must push yourself to stay on top of your assignments and ahead in your studies. Law school is expensive and you should look at the money you are spending on law school as your salary, a salary that must be earned by hard work and perseverance. When people ask you what you do for a living you should be proud to say, "I'm a law student."

> **SIDEBAR:** One of the biggest mistakes I made was to go directly from a master's program to law school without taking a break in between. To put it another way, I went from summer semester studies in graduate school to fall semester studies in law school. This was a BIG MISTAKE! Be sure to take some time off, at least a couple of months, before starting law school. Go to the beach, read a trashy novel, follow a band around, or just lay around relaxing. Your brain will need the break because it is in for quite a shock come the first day of your legal studies.

SIDEBAR: If at all possible, arrive in the town or city that your law school is located in a month or two before classes start. Find a place to live as close to the law school as possible that is affordable and safe. If you want to live on campus, check with your law school about graduate housing for law students. Regardless of whether you live on campus or not, you might want to check with your school about on-campus meal plans, so you won't have to worry about cooking. On campus meal plans are often cheaper than buying lunch every day at the local delis and restaurants. Take some time to get to know your way around the campus and the town or city it is located in. This will be your home for the next 3 years, so take some time to get to know it. By arriving early for law school, it will help take the stress out of finding a place to live, learning your way around campus, and assuming your new role as a law student.

THE LAW SCHOOL ENVIRONMENT

If you hated high school and think that law school is going to be a scholarly paradise where people are respected for their minds, you might want to think again. Most law schools are relatively small in size, with class sizes and an overall enrollment similar in size to the typical American high school. Needless to say, it is more likely than not that your law school classmates are going to know your name, your personality, and whether or not you are in the top 10% of the class. It is simply the nature of a small school environment. This small school nature is only magnified by the competitive nature of law school, so knowing the type of people that typically inhabit this environment will only help you to successfully survive and thrive in such an environment.

Law Professors. There is an old saying in law school that the students that graduate in the top 10% of their class go onto be law professors, the students that graduate in the top 20% go onto be judges, the students that graduate in the top 30–50% make the best lawyers, and the students that graduate in the lower 50% make the most money. The validity of much of this saying is debatable, especially in a state were judges are elected and who you know often matters more than what you know, however, the statement's validity does seem to hold true for law professors, as it is a rarity to find a law professor who is not a former top 10%'er. In fact, it has been my experience that many law professors have no trouble conveying to their students the fact that they finished in the top 10% of their class. To that end, you should not be surprised to find that many of your law professors are a little bit arrogant or even egotistic, as they have aspired to and obtained the esteemed position of teacher of the law. Regardless of the amount of arrogance or egotism a law professor might display, each professor is deserving of your respect and you will find that if you make the effort to be respectful to each of your professors, many, if not all, of them will make the effort to be respectful of you as a student and a future member of the legal profession.

SIDEBAR: One of the easiest ways to show respect to a law professor or any professor is to be on time to class and not skip class. Also, make an effort to engage your professors outside of the classroom in conversations that don't necessarily involve the law. Often times, students that make an effort to know their professors outside of the classroom are surprised to find that their professors have the same or similar interests that they do. Professors also tend to remember more highly those students who took the time to get to know them outside the classroom when it comes time to give job recommendations and references.

SIDEBAR: Try not to judge a professor by your experience on the first day of class. Many professors like to put the fear of law school and the Professor Almighty into first year law students. Reserve your judgment of a professor until after the first month or two of classes because many times a class that appears on the first day as if it is going to be your most hated class often times turns out to be your most enjoyable, due in no small part to the professor's teaching ability.

Law School Staff. From the janitor to the librarian to the office secretaries, the members of the law school staff are the ones that run the day-to-day operations of the law school. The law school staff, like all people, need to be treated with dignity and respect. Do not be afraid to say "hello" to the janitor or chat with the secretary while you are waiting in an office. In fact, you should make it a point to be known by the law school staff as a student that is friendly and respectful.

SIDEBAR: Do not make the unfortunate mistake that some law students do when they first get their law school acceptance letter of thinking that their status as a law student somehow elevates them above the status of other people. I like to call this the Big Head Syndrome, a disease of unjustified arrogance that can severely handicap a law student without him or her knowing it. The law in America is about equality and law students should remember this when dealing with the law school staff. The law school staff deserves to be treated as your equals and not your servants. The law school staff is there to make your law school experience a little bit easier and a lot more enjoyable. Make the law school staff your friends and you will be playing it smart but make the law school staff your enemies and you will be making a stupid, stupid mistake.

SIDEBAR: Some members of the law school staff that you might want to be particularly nice to are the ones that staff the registration office and the job placement office. When you find yourself having trouble with your class schedule or law school transcript or wanting to get on the on-campus interview list after the deadline, having a friendly face to talk to will serve you well. A kind word on Secretary's Day or holidays will take you further than scowling and yelling at a staff member when something doesn't go the way you think it should or want it to.

Law School Students. Law students come from all walks of life. Some are minorities, some are women, some are men, some are married, some are single, some are non-traditional students looking for a second career, some are arrogant, some are just plain narcissistic, and some may even be teenage geniuses. Most are used to being at or near the top of their class and most are heading for the disappointment of learning that the A's they were used to getting as an undergraduate have been replaced with B's and C's that they are now relieved to be getting. All are your classmates and all are under a tremendous amount of stress. You don't have to learn to like them but you do have to learn to get along with them.

SIDEBAR: The legal profession is a profession that is based not only on the law but personal interactions, be it interactions between two lawyers, a lawyer and a judge, a lawyer and the jury, or a lawyer and his or her client. Consequently, you need to learn to foster professional relationships with your classmates and learn how to get along with people who possess different beliefs and views than you do. Don't isolate yourself in the law library or your bedroom studying all the time but make an effort to socialize with your classmates and get to know them both inside and outside the law school. No man or woman ever had too many friends.

THE LAW SCHOOL ROUTINE

This section is intended to provide you with a set of survival tips, both study tips and general tips, to make your law school life a more enjoyable and fulfilling experience. The order that the survival tips appear in below is no indication of their importance, as the information contained in each tip is important, but simply indicates an order in which you might experience a situation in law school that is covered by the survival tip.

1. Go to your law school orientation and pay attention. Most law schools have at least a one or two day orientation for all incoming first year law students. Do not skip this orientation but show up with a good attitude and pay attention. Orientation is when the law school lets you know how things work with regard to such things as class scheduling and conflicts. Orientation is also the time that most law schools issue students their law school ID's, computer passwords, and study cubicles, as well as give students a chance to meet some of their professors and fellow students for the first time.

2. Know your title and place. In law school, first year students are called "1L's," second year students are called "2L's," and third year students are called "3L's." As for knowing your place, just keep in mind that at most law schools, 1L's are the last to be allowed to register for classes each semester or quarter and only after 2L's and 3L's have had an opportunity to register.

3. Know what you are in law school to learn. Contrary to popular belief, you do not go to law school to learn the law, as learning every aspect of the law would be an impossible feat because the law is constantly changing. You go to law school to learn to think like a lawyer. The sooner you grasp this concept the sooner law school will start to make more sense to you. Do not worry about memorizing every word of the *United States Constitution* but worry about how it affects peoples' lives and how it can be used to solve their legal problems.

> **SIDEBAR:** In your journey as a law student, you will soon learn that many times when one is dealing with the law there is no black or white answer but only a confusing shade of gray and justice is often times in the eye of the beholder. If this concept of the law seems to trample on your ideals of fair play, don't let it. The law is a wonderful tool that American society uses to solve its conflicts peacefully. With the law, many times a lawyer is working to arrive at the answer of, "maybe." Simply put, a lawyer is trained to look at a set of facts and predict what will happen in the legal system, taking into account all possible scenarios. This often results in a lawyer giving his or her client an answer of, "maybe if these factors are present." If you are able to grasp the concept that you are in law school to learn how to get to "maybe" when it comes to the law, you will find you are beginning to think like a lawyer and your law school exams won't be as intimidating.

4. Student handbook. Most law schools provide 1L's with a student handbook. Take the time to read this handbook, you won't regret that you did.

5. Honor code. Most law schools have an honor code to ensure academic honesty. Learn this honor code and take it seriously because your professors and classmates will be taking it seriously.

6. Use your mentor. Many law schools assign 1L's a 2L or 3L as a mentor for the 1L to learn from. If your law school assigns you a mentor, make an effort to meet with your mentor on a regular basis and learn from him or her.

> **SIDEBAR:** The University of Missouri-Columbia's School of Law assigns 1L's mentors and I sincerely regret not taking advantage of this program. I cannot help but think that had I taken the time to meet with my mentor he could have clued me in on how the law school operated and what to expect as far as classes, professors, and exams were concerned. Use your mentor, it could mean the difference between finishing in the top 10% of your class and finishing in the bottom 50%.

7. Check for first-day-of-class assignments. A favorite thing for law professors to do is to have an assignment due the first day of class each semester, especially when it involves a class populated by 1L's. Always check for first-day-of-class assignments each semester, this includes your very first semester of law school. In other words, don't be surprised if you have an assignment due your very first day of law school. Welcome to law school! Most law schools have an assignment board for class assignments and/or post class assignments on the school's web page, which is an Internet address you need to commit to memory and visit on a regular basis.

8. Law books. Law books are expensive and your first trip to the school bookstore may be a rather painful experience. Due to the fact that the loss incurred on the reselling of law books back to the school bookstore is so great, many law students simply keep their law books instead of selling them back. Keeping your law books is an excellent way to begin to compile a law reference library that every lawyer worth his or her salt has in their office. If you are looking to save money, many school bookstores and online booksellers offer used law books but be sure you are getting the right edition of the book that is assigned. Also, it is best if you can inspect the used book before purchasing it to ensure that the book is not damaged to the point of being of no real use to you. Remember, most law students highlight, as well as write (i.e. take notes) on, the pages of the books they sell back.

SIDEBAR: Don't be fooled into thinking that you need to buy one of those big, expensive law dictionaries. A pocket-sized law dictionary will do just fine and your school's law library should have no shortage of big, expensive law dictionaries on hand for you to use. Don't be fooled, however, into thinking you can get by without buying a law dictionary. The study of the law is unlike anything else and the law has its own terminology that you must become familiar with if you are to succeed as a law student and a lawyer. Also, if your school assigns you a locker, don't be afraid to use it because there is no reason to haul your law books back and forth from home to school each day, especially if you are showing up early and staying late.

SIDEBAR: When you are purchasing your law books, always check to see if there is a corresponding study guide or workbook being offered for sale along with the book. I had a professor in law school that always taught from law books whose authors had also written a study guide or workbook to supplement the book. I always bought these supplemental materials because often times I found myself at first not understanding a word my professor was saying in class or that I was reading in the law book but did understand after working through the supplemental study guide or workbook.

SIDEBAR: I am a big proponent of highlighting and taking notes in the pages of law books, as it is easier to keep track of a book than a piece of paper. Consequently, I recommend purchasing new law books, as a way of ensuring that all the marks and notes in the books are yours and are relevant to the classes you are using the books for. The book publishers should love this sidebar.

9. Go to class. You are paying far too much money for a law school education to be skipping classes. If you are treating being a law student like your job, you should have no problem showing up for each and every class. The busy schedule you keep in law school will help prepare you for the busy schedule you will be asked to keep as a new associate at a law firm or newly hired attorney at a state or federal agency.

SIDEBAR: Going to class sometimes has unexpected benefits. Many times in law school, I had professors who were so frustrated about the number of people who were not in attendance that they gave a pop quiz in which the answer was obvious or even written on the classroom's blackboard (i.e. everybody was going to get 100%) or gave everyone in attendance bonus points simply for signing their names to a piece of notebook paper that the professor passed around the class. Bonus points can go a long way when it comes to your final grade in a class. Many law schools also have an attendance policy dictating how many unexcused absences a student can have without being penalized. Many professors enforce the law school's attendance policy or impose an even harsher one on their classes.

10. Take good notes. When you go to class, don't just sit there like a bump on a log; take good notes! Often times the professor will flat out tell you what is going to be on a final exam, so taking good notes will ensure that you have this valuable information at the end of the semester when exams roll around. Taking good notes also helps you to better understand the legal concepts the professor is trying to teach you.

SIDEBAR: With the explosion of technology over the last two decades, some law students prefer to take notes directly on their laptop computers than by the traditional method of pen on paper. If you are like me and type too slow to keep up with the professor, I would recommend taking notes with pen and paper and then transcribing your notes on the computer into outline form after class.

SIDEBAR: Though they are getting smaller and smaller all the time, laptops often prove bulky and hard to keep up with in law school. Most law schools provide computer labs for their students and I would recommend that students wanting portable computer power outside these labs consider Palm Pilots or handheld computers. The memory capability on these machines is now to the point that they can support programs such as Microsoft Word and are much smaller than laptops and easier to carry back and forth to law school. Portable, fold up keyboards are also available to use with these machines and make data entry much easier. The machines can also be used to store law school information, such as class schedules and phone numbers.

11. Keep your outlines updated. The main method that law students use to study for exams is by outlines that are created from their classroom notes. Consequently, you need to keep up with your outlines because many times outlines end up being over 50-pages at the end of the semester and it is much easier to create an outline as the semester progresses than it is to create one a week before your final exams. This aspect of law school is so important that this book contains an entire set of survival tips dedicated solely to outlines.

12. Make a study schedule. Most successful law students have a study schedule that they strictly adhere to. I recommend creating a study schedule that allows you to get everything you need to get done before the weekend because you need time to unwind every week and not think about law school. In other words, your 50–70 hours per week law school job should be scheduled for Monday through Friday, which usually entails getting to work early and going home late. Live at the law school during the week but get as far away from it as you can on the weekends.

SIDEBAR: Part of your daily study schedule should include time to transcribe your class notes into outlines using a computer program such as Microsoft Word or Word Perfect. I cannot stress the importance enough of staying on top of your outline production.

SIDEBAR: The best place I found to study in law school was in the law library. This environment is one that is conducive to study, as opposed to one's home environment that often times proves very distracting. It is hard to concentrate on the law and watch *Monday Night Football* or sitcoms at the same time. Staying at the law school for 10–12 hours a day might involve bringing your breakfast, lunch, and dinner with you but it will prove worth it in the long run.

13. Come prepared for class. American law schools teach their students using the casebook method. Simply translated, law students learn the law by reading and understanding books full of court decisions, which results in law students being asked to read a lot of court cases. To ensure that their students are keeping up with their reading assignments, law professors frequently call upon students to recite the facts of, or the court's holding (ruling) in, a particular case. Don't be the student left stammering and stuttering when the professor calls upon you for an answer. Keep ahead in your reading assignments and you will keep ahead in the class rankings. Also, don't be afraid to make notes in the margins of those expensive law books.

SIDEBAR: Many law professors use a seating chart to learn students' names, as well as keep track of how many times a student has been called on in class. Everybody will have to face the music some day and being prepared for class will help ease your anxiety and stress levels. Professors also seem particularly found of calling on students sitting in the back row, so choose your seat on the first day of class wisely. Being called on during a law school class if very stressful, as you are being put on the spot in front of your fellow law students and future peers, so do not make it more stressful than it has to be by coming to class unprepared.

SIDEBAR: If you haven't prepared for class and are called upon, it is better to come right out and own up to the fact that you are not prepared than it is to try and pretend that you are. A simple, "Professor, I'm sorry but I am not prepared today" may get you chided for slacking off but woe be to the student who wastes the professor's time trying to smooth talk his or her way out of being caught unprepared. Also, telling the professor before class that you are not prepared may earn you a pass for the day and the professor's respect for not wasting his or her time but, if I were you, I would make sure I came to the next class extra prepared. You may be surprised how far a simple "yes sir" or "no mam" or the display of common courtesy towards your professors might go in making your law school experience a more enjoyable one. Plus, as future legal professionals, displaying courtesy toward others should be a regular occurrence and not the exception.

14. Don't be afraid to raise that hand. Law school is an expensive endeavor to undertake and you should not be afraid to raise your hand and ask questions of your professors. If you don't understand something the professor is talking about, raise your hand and ask the professor to explain it better. Law professors are experts in the subjects that they teach and sometimes forget that concepts that seem simple to them may not seem that simple to their students. I have yet to meet a law professor who was unwilling to answer a student's question, even if it was a stupid one because there are no stupid questions just people that remain ignorant out of fear of asking one. Also, do not be afraid to approach your professors before or after class with questions. Most professors also have regularly scheduled office hours during which students can stop by for extra help. Do not be afraid to stick your head into a professor's office during office hours and ask for help. It's your tuition money; don't waste it by being shy. You are going into the wrong profession to remain shy.

SIDEBAR: There is one question I would caution you against asking a law professor and that is, "Where would you draw the line when it comes to that area of the law?" I had the misfortune to ask this question on my first day of class as a 1L and the professor proceeded to answer it by drawing a line on the blackboard with a piece of chalk and saying, "there." The law is often relative and many times lines have not been drawn by the courts, so asking a law professor to say where he or she would draw the line when it comes to the law will often times get you the same response I got on my first day of law school.

15. Get to know your classmates. Don't be afraid to get to know your classmates, they are your future colleagues. Also, you may be surprised by how many of your classmates are second or third generation law students that have access to very useful information, such as what firms are hiring for summer internships and what judge is looking for a clerk. Remember, your classmates are facing the same trials and tribulations you are and might enjoy meeting a new friend.

> **SIDEBAR:** Your law school classmates can be very helpful when it comes to deciding what classes to take in your second and third year of law school and what professors, if any, to avoid. Don't be surprised if one of your classmates has an old class outline or copy of a past exam that he or she is willing to share with you just because you're a friend. Like books in the law library, your classmates are a resource in and of themselves that can help make your time in law school an easier and more successful experience.

16. Take a class in every bar exam subject. It is a popular practice in law school to advise students that they do not have to take a class in every subject that is on a state's bar exam to pass the exam. This is true but, having learned the hard way how difficult it is to study for a bar exam subject that I didn't have a class on in law school, I would advise every law student to defy conventional wisdom and take a class in every subject on the bar exam. Take it from me, it is a lot easier to study a bar exam subject once you have had a class on it.

> **SIDEBAR:** Most law schools have a mandatory set of classes that all 1L's have to take, so it is more likely than not that you won't have to worry about registering for classes until it comes time to register for your 2L classes. Aside from taking a class in every subject covered on a state's bar exam, I would advise students to take elective classes in areas of the law they are planning to practice in, as well as take a history of the *United States Constitution* class, due to the fact that all lawyers need to know the history of the highest law of the land.

> **SIDEBAR:** Your law school should be able to provide you with a list of subjects that are covered on a state's bar exam, if not, a visit to that state's government or courts web pages should be able to provide you with bar exam information. Also, the BAR/BRI web page at www.barbri.com routinely lists each state's bar exam subjects.

17. Get organized and stay organized. Law school is not the place to be having papers hanging loose out of folders. Get organized and stay organized because you will have a lot of assignments and due dates to keep track of. If you don't have calendar or daily planner get one, preferably one that allows you to view a full month at a time so you know what assignments and due dates are coming up.

18. Save every piece of paper you get from the law school. Save every piece of paper that you get from the law school that looks like it is even remotely important. At the very least store the papers in a shoebox under your bed. You won't be the first law student whose transcript contained wrong information and you will be glad you have a record of your law school activities to help resolve any disputes and correct any errors involving your transcript or other law school records.

19. Embrace technology. The day of the typewriter is over, so if you have yet to learn how to use a computer do so immediately. More and more courts are going to computer-based recordkeeping and docketing systems and more and more legal research is being done on computers. Don't find yourself stuck in the 20th century while your law school and classmates are embracing and using 21st century technology.

20. Keep up with what is going on in your law school community. Keep up with the events that are being sponsored by and going on at your law school. Make it a point to go to these events and make your presence known in your law school community. You will enjoy law school more if you feel like you are part of your law school community.

SIDEBAR: Many times activities sponsored by the law school or student organizations will be designed as a way for students to get together and socialize, as well as get away from their studies for awhile. Activities such as movie night where students meet to watch classic law movies like the *Paper Chase* and *My Cousin Vinny* and happy hour gatherings held at different local watering holes, affectionately referred to by many students as The Bar Review, are common occurrences at law schools. Make an effort to attend some of these social gatherings and get to know your classmates outside of the law school. Who knows, you may even run into some of your professors out enjoying themselves.

21. Stay focused and stay positive. Stay focused on your law studies by staying positive. Law school is a struggle for most students and many tend to develop a negative attitude about law school and their lives in general. Don't let the negative attitude of others influence you. Stay positive and embrace the learning adventure that is law school. A positive mental outlook will help make law school a more enjoyable experience.

22. Things can walk off in law school. Most law schools are open to the public and other students. Consequently, be careful what you leave laying around the law school lest your laptop should find its way to an undergraduate biology class or even worse, a classmate's house or apartment.

23. Remember that all that money has to be paid back. All the money that you borrow to go to law school has to be paid back someday. For those of you with undergraduate debt, as well as law school debt, this amount can get pretty high pretty fast. Try to save money whenever possible and never stop looking for scholarships, grants, and internships that will help you pay for law school. Sharing an apartment with one or more of your classmates, walking or riding a bike to school, carpooling, and taking your lunch are all good ways to save money in law school. Making a budget and sticking to it is still the best way to save money both in law school and out. When making your budget remember that there are things that a law student can do without, such as cable, tanning salons, private gyms, and expensive spring break getaways.

24. Write down your goals for law school. Some of the best advice I ever got was to write down my goals. There is something about writing down your goals that helps you better achieve them. I think it has something to do with the feeling one gets when he or she checks off a completed project from a "to do" list. No goal is too small or too big. If you want to finish in the top 10% of your class, write it down as one of your goals. If you want to never skip a class the entire time you are in law school than write it down as one of your goals. Write your goals down and you will be amazed how it helps your overall focus and attitude on law school.

25. Don't forget about the outside world. Law students have a tendency to forget about the world outside the law school. Don't forget about the outside world. Pickup a newspaper every now and then and take the time to read it through. Virtually everything that goes on in the world is affected by the law or has an effect on the law, so keep up with the outside world and stay in tune with what is going on with the law out there.

SIDEBAR: A great way to keep up with events in America's legal community is to read *Lawyers Weekly USA*, a newspaper published for lawyers. In addition to the national newspaper there are also state newspapers published by Lawyers Weekly, Inc., for Massachusetts, Michigan, Missouri, North Carolina, Ohio, Rhode Island, South Carolina, and Virginia. Your law school library should receive at least a copy of the national newspaper *Lawyers Weekly USA*. More information on Lawyers Weekly, Inc., can be found at www.lawyersweekly.com.

26. DON'T MAKE A STUPID MISTAKE. As a law student, you are in the beginning stages of your law career. Do not jeopardize this career by making a stupid mistake while in law school, such as being convicted of drunk driving or drug possession, it could end your career before it even gets started. Most employers, both private and governmental, do extensive background checks as part of their hiring process. Consequently, a stupid mistake in law school will often translate itself into an embarrassing disclosure on a job application and an abrupt end to a job interview.

SIDEBAR: Undoubtedly, at some point during your 3 year long journey through law school you will be asked to attend a party or social function where alcohol will be served. Watch yourself, as you wouldn't be the first law school student who has ever been arrested and convicted of drunk driving. Drunk driving is a stupid mistake that can cost you dearly as a law student and endangers your life and the life of others. If you are attending a party or social function where alcohol is being served, please take a cab or have a designated driver. Also, drug convictions can be absolutely devastating to a law career, as most state and federal agencies will not hire a person with a drug conviction. Ask yourself before taking an illegal substance if the risk of ending your law career before it even gets started is worth the momentary pleasure the drug will bring you. If you think you have a problem with drugs or alcohol, please seek help and take the steps necessary to address your problem before the problem ends up costing you more than you ever imagined it could.

22

CASE BRIEFS

One exercise that many law schools like to make a part of thei̇   ̲̲̲̲uons is to have incoming students prepare a formal brief of an actual court case or two. A case brief should be no more than one to two pages in length and should contain the name of the court in which the case was decided, the name of the case, the case citation, names of the parties involved, the facts, the issue(s) decided, the court's decision (holding), and the legal authority the court relied on in reaching its decision. The case of <u>McCabe v. Director of Revenue, State of Missouri</u>, 7 S.W.3d 12 (Mo.App. E.D. 1999), will be used to illustrate how to properly construct a case brief.

7 S.W.3d 12
Missouri Court of Appeals, Eastern District, Division Four
Kevin James McCabe, Respondent,
v.
Director of Revenue, State of Missouri, Appellant

WILLIAM H. CRANDALL, Jr., Presiding Judge.

The Director of Revenue (Director) appeals from the judgment reinstating Kevin McCabe's driving privileges. We reverse and remand.

On September 25, 1997, a St. Louis County police officer arrested McCabe for driving while intoxicated. According to the officer, McCabe refused to submit to a breath test. Director notified McCabe that pursuant to section 577.041 RSMO Cum.Supp.1997, his driving privileges would be revoked for one year for refusing to submit to a breath test. McCabe filed a petition for review of the revocation in St. Louis County Circuit Court.

At trial, Director offered an exhibit that included in part an Alcohol Influence Report signed by the arresting officer[1]. McCabe objected to a portion of the report. The commissioner took the objection under advisement. Director offered no additional evidence and McCabe offered no evidence. The commissioner found that the arresting officer did not see McCabe operating the motor vehicle and did not have probable cause to arrest McCabe. The commissioner also found that McCabe did not refuse to take the breath test. The commissioner recommended that the circuit court reinstate McCabe's driving

---

1.   The record does not reflect that the exhibit was offered pursuant to section 302.312 RSMO Cum.Supp.1997 or section 490.692 RSMO 1994.

privileges. The circuit court signed the commissioner's findings and recommendations as the judgment of the court. Director appeals from this judgment.

The judgment will be affirmed unless there is no substantial evidence to support it, it is against the weight of the evidence, or it erroneously declares or applies that law. *Tharp v. Director of Revenue,* 969 S.W.2d 330, 331 (Mo.App. E.D. 1998). In a proceeding where a person's license has been revoked for refusal to submit to a breath test, the trial court shall determine (1) whether the person was arrested, (2) whether the arresting officer had reasonable grounds to believe that the person was driving a motor vehicle while in an intoxicated condition, and (3) whether or not the person refused to submit to the test. Section 577.041.4 RSMO Cum.Supp.1997; *Harder v. Director of Revenue,* 969 S.W.2d 340, 341 (Mo.App. E.D. 1998).

The parties do not dispute that the officer arrested McCabe. We first address the court's finding that the arresting officer did not have probable cause to arrest McCabe for driving while intoxicated. Attached to the Alcohol Influence Report is a page titled "NARRATIVE INFORMATION." A part of the "NARRATIVE INFORMATION" provides certain statements by the arresting officer regarding the circumstances prior to McCabe's arrest. The arresting officer states:

> I responded to a call to meet an off duty officer—who stated that while traveling south on Bellefontaine, he observed a 1996 Jeep Cherokee, black in color occupied by one white male, to be swerving back and forth across the center line. [The off duty officer] further stated that at the intersection of Bellefontaine and Larimore he passed the black Cherokee on the left and continued south on Bellefontaine...The driver of the black Cherokee later identified as Kevin McCabe, then accelerated and got directly behind [the off duty officer]. Due to the erratic driving of Kevin McCabe [the off duty officer] pulled to the right and stopped on the shoulder of Bellefontaine at the intersection of Dunn, in an effort to allow Kevin to pass. Kevin then came to an abrupt stop directly behind [the off duty officer] and stated [an obscenity.] [The off duty officer] then ordered Kevin to pull his vehicle to the curb, to which he complied. Kevin exited his vehicle and then began to yell obscenities...[The off duty officer] advised me that he believed due to the subject[']s driving that he was under the influence of alcohol.

The arresting officer also states in the "NARRATIVE INFORMATION" that while interviewing McCabe he could smell the odor of alcohol coming from McCabe's breath and that McCabe refused to participate in a field sobriety test. The officer then arrested McCabe.

At trial, McCabe objected, on the basis of hearsay, to the admission of the statements made by the off duty officer to the arresting officer. However, "hearsay evidence is sufficient to establish probable cause because it is not offered for its truth, but to explain the basis for [a] belief that probable cause to arrest existed." *State v. Holt*, 695 S.W.2d 474, 478 (Mo.App. 1985). The off duty officer's statements to the arresting officer were therefore admissible to determine if there was probable cause to arrest.

The court found that the arresting officer did not see McCabe operating the motor vehicle and then found that the officer did not have probable cause to arrest McCabe for driving while intoxicated. Probable cause exists when the facts and circumstances would warrant a reasonable person to believe that an offense has been committed. *Farin v. Director of Revenue*, 982 S.W.2d 712, 715 (Mo.App. E.D. 1998). A determination of whether an officer had probable cause to make an arrest must be made in relation to the circumstances as they would have appeared to a prudent, cautious and trained police officer. *Id.*

Here, the off duty officer observed McCabe driving and other actions of McCabe. The arresting officer smelled alcohol on McCabe's breath. It is not necessary for an officer to actually observe a person driving to have probable cause to arrest the person for driving while intoxicated. *Id.* at 714–15; *Chinnery v. Director of Revenue*, 885 S.W.2d 50, 51 (Mo.App. W.D. 1994). Probable cause is determined by the collective knowledge and facts available to all of the officers participating in the arrest. *Farin*, 982 S.W.2d at 715. "The arresting officer does not need to possess all of the information." *Id.* Furthermore, a police officer is entitled to rely on official information provided by another officer when determining if there is probable cause to arrest. *Id.* The evidence provided in the "NARRATIVE INFORMATION" was sufficient to establish that the arresting officer had probable cause to arrest McCabe for driving while intoxicated. McCabe presented no evidence at trial. The court's finding that the officer did not have probable cause to arrest McCabe for driving while intoxicated is against the weight of the evidence and is not supported by substantial evidence.

We next address the court's findings that McCabe did not refuse the breath test. A part of the "NARRATIVE INFORMATION" contains the arresting officer's statement that McCabe refused to submit to a chemical test of his breath. The Alcohol Influence Report also has a section that the officer must mark if the arrested person refuses to submit to a chemical test of their alcohol content. Here, the officer marked the appropriate box. Because McCabe did not object to any of these portions of the Alcohol Influence Report, this evidence should be considered in determining whether or not McCabe refused to submit to the breath test. *Reinert v. Director of Revenue*, 894 S.W.2d 162, 164 (Mo. banc, 1995). As previously stated, McCabe offered no evidence at trial. The court's findings that McCabe did not refuse to submit to the breath test is against the weight of the evidence and is not supported by substantial evidence.

The judgment is reversed and the cause remanded with directions to reinstate the Director's revocation of McCabe's driving privileges.

KENT E. KAROHL, J. and MARY K. HOFF, J., Concur.

SIDEBAR: Congratulations to all of you who have just finished reading your first court case. You may not realize it yet but you have just taken a big step towards becoming a lawyer.

Case Brief: McCabe v. DOR

Court:	Missouri Court of Appeals—Eastern District
Parties:	Kevin James McCabe—Respondent
	Director of Revenue, State of Missouri—Appellant
Citation:	7 S.W.3d 12
Date:	October 5, 1999

Facts:

1. McCabe was stopped by an off duty police officer.

2. Arresting officer responded to a call to meet the off duty officer.

3. Arresting officer learns from off duty officer that McCabe was swerving back and forth across the centerline.

4. McCabe's arrest based on the off duty officer's observations and the fact that McCabe's breath smelled of alcohol.

5. Alcohol Influence Report indicated that McCabe refused to take a breath test.

6. McCabe's driving privileges were revoked for one year by DOR.

Trial Court's Decision: Arresting officer did not see McCabe driving, and therefore; the arresting officer did not have probable cause to arrest McCabe. Additionally, there was no evidence that McCabe refused to take a breath test. McCabe's driving privileges reinstated.

Issue(s) On Appeal: (1) Whether probable cause existed to arrest McCabe?, and (2) Whether there was evidence that McCabe refused to take a breath test?

Court's Holding: The arresting officer did not have to see McCabe driving to establish probable cause to arrest him for DWI and the Alcohol Influence Report contained evidence that McCabe refused to take a breath test. The trial court's decision is reverse and remanded with instructions to reinstate the revocation of McCabe's driving privileges.

Legal Authority Relied On:

—<u>Chinnery v. Director of Revenue</u>, 885 S.W.2d 50 (Mo.App. W.D. 1994)—Arresting officer does not have to see a driver driving to arrest the driver for DWI.

—<u>Farin v. Director of Revenue</u>, 982 S.W.2d 712 (Mo.App. E.D. 1998)—Probable cause is determined by collective knowledge. Arresting officer can rely on information from another officer to establish probable cause.

—<u>Reinert v. Director of Revenue</u>, 894 S.W.2d 162 (Mo. banc 1995)—Alcohol Influence Report is evidence that should be considered when determining whether a driver refused to take a breath test.

SIDEBAR: Some of the disadvantages of doing a formal case brief for every case you read in law school are that it can be very time consuming and it can leave you with a lot of extra paper to keep track of. Consequently, unless you just feel more comfortable doing formal case briefs or are required to do formal briefs for a class, I would recommend briefing cases in the side margins of your casebooks after you have become proficient at creating formal briefs. As I said before, books are easier to keep track of than paper and are a financial loss when it comes to their resale value, so you should feel free to go ahead and mark them up with notes in the margins. Having your case briefs in the margins of your books will give you one less thing to worry about, namely, where your case briefs are.

SIDEBAR: Highlighters can be very dangerous things in law school. As a 1L, I found myself highlighting virtually everything I thought looked important in a case and ended up with a lot of book pages that looked almost completely yellow. To avoid highlighter mania, be sure to read the case through one time before you highlight anything. After you have read the case through once, go back and highlight a few helpful facts and the court's holding, this will keep you from having pages full of yellow ink.

SIDEBAR: If you find that you are more comfortable, at least during the first year of law school, doing formal case briefs, I recommend that you make a computer template for your briefs that you can type the case information in or at least print off and fill in by hand, similar to a fill-in-the-blank worksheet.

CLASS OUTLINES

Just as the name implies, class outlines are outlines, very detailed outlines derived from class notes that law students create to study for end-of-the-semester final exams. The last few pages of this section is an example of an actual law school outline prepared for an Estates & Trusts class but before you see what an actual law school outline should look like take the time to read over the following list of survival tips concerning outlines:

1. Commercial outlines are worth the money. One of the worst things I ever did in law school was to take the advice of a law professor at orientation who told me that I didn't need to waste my money on commercial outlines because, according to the professor, if I took good notes in class I would be able to create my own outlines with relative ease. Contrary to the professor's advice, I had difficulty creating my own outlines or even deciding what form to put my outlines in. Commercial outlines can help you better understand what is going on in your classes, as well as help give you an idea of what your own outlines should look like.

SIDEBAR: Although I highly recommend using commercial outlines in your law school studies, it is imperative that you prepare your own outlines for each class you have in law school, as it is one the most effective ways to learn the law. Also, the law is constantly changing, which always leaves open that possibility that your commercial outlines no longer contain valid information on one or more aspects of the law and you may find your professors are fond of testing you over parts of the law that they know most commercial outlines do not cover. Some professors are just crazy like that, wanting you to come to their classes and all. Go figure.

SIDEBAR: You should use your commercial outlines much like you use your law books. In other words, don't be afraid to take your commercial outlines to class and make notes in the margins, especially when one of your professors tells you that you should expect to see something again on the final exam.

SIDEBAR: Gilberts and Emanuel are well-respected names in the commercial outline business but they are not the only names, so shop around for the commercial outlines that you like best. If you are having trouble locating commercial outlines that you like in your law school bookstore, you might try shopping for outlines at online bookstores, such as amazon.com and barnesandnoble.com.

---

2. Keep your outlines up to date. If you ignore all the other survival tips I give you on outlines, do not ignore this one. Try to work on your outlines from day one of classes. Look at the example provided at the end of this section or commercial outlines to get an idea of how to format your outlines if you feel you don't know how or where to start an outline. Believe me, a little bit of typing after class is much better than a lot of typing at the end of the semester.

SIDEBAR: When preparing your class outlines on the computer, be sure to periodically back your work up on a floppy disk or CD because there is nothing like that sinking feeling in the pit of your stomach when you realize that all of your hard work is lost somewhere in the circuitry of your computer. Remember, a well prepared outline can help you review for the bar exam when that times comes and having them conveniently stored on a floppy disk or CD will prove useful.

---

3. Keep an eye out for that certain guy or gal. Without fail, there is always a guy or gal in every law school class that has somehow managed to get his or her hands on outstanding class outlines from previous years, be it from earlier law school graduates, a long lost uncle, or as a result of a lucky dive in the dumpster behind the law school. Find out who this classmate is and see if you can't get a copy of his or her outlines or at least a look at them because it can help you with ideas on how to format your own outlines, as well as provide you with some possible clues to what might be on a professor's final exam.

SIDEBAR: Don't be surprised if an outline possessing classmate charges you a small fee to look at his or her outlines. You pay for commercial outlines and some of your classmates you will soon learn may not be as big hearted as you. If your school has a mentor program, don't forget to ask your mentor if he or she has any good outlines laying around. Also, don't be afraid to become that guy or gal when it comes to creating good outlines. Whether you charge your fellow law students for your expertise is entirely up to you but just remember what goes around usually comes around.

SIDEBAR: Another good source of outlines is law school clubs and organizations, such as the Women's Law Association (WLA) and the Federalist Society. In fact, during law school I affectionately referred to the WLA at the University of Missouri-Columbia's School of Law as the law school mafia because of their reputation for supplying their members with some of the best outlines available in law school.

---

4. Lists. If your professor gives you a list of cases, laws, vocabulary words, or items and tells you that you should remember the list for the final exam make sure the list finds its way into your outline and into your brain before the exam.

5. Do not try and understand the example outline. Do not worry about understanding the example outline from the Estates and Trusts class unless you have had such a class. The example outline is not intended to be a study guide but a tool to give you an idea of what your class outlines should look like.

Example Of An Actual Law Outline From An Estates & Trusts Class

Wills

I. Intestacy

    1. Surviving spouse (S-spouse)

        • All of the estate if no issue

        • 1st 20K + ½ of remainder estate, if all issues of the S-spouse

        • ½ estate if issue but some are not issue of the S-spouse

    2. Issue = per capita with representation

    3. Ancestors and Collaterals

        • Parents & Siblings = per capita only surviving (equal shares)

        • Grandparents, Aunts, Uncles = per capita only surviving

        • Rule against remoteness

    4. Relative of spouse = only if no one in Decedent's (D) family.

    5. Escheat = only if no survivors in D's or SS's family

    —Relationships

        • Adopted child = real child

        • Child born out of wedlock = Mother's child unless:

            1. Marriage at any time before or after birth, or

            2. Adjudication

                —If 1 or 2 happen = child is child of father as well

        • Father can take from child unless:

            1. Did not act like father, or

            2. Adjudication

        • Halfbloods = take ½ share

—Time of relationship

  • Divorce = spouse is cutoff (treated as predeceased)

  • Posthumous heir = 280 day presumption

  • 120 hour survival statute

—Disqualifications

  • Remoteness

  • Paternity by adjudication

  • Intentional killer

  • Spousal conduct:

        1. Abandonment without cause for a year, or

        2. Separation and then adultery

  • Waiver by marital agreement:

        1. Written contract, and

        2. Full disclosure of rights being waived, and

        3. Fair considerations

—Property Subject To Intestate Succession:

  • Gross probate = all rights owned by the D

  • Net Probate Estate = GPE - (exempt property, support & homestead allowance)

  • Advancement = only wholly intestate

II. Requirements

  1. Formality

    • Written or oral (only if made in imminent peril of death, death from that peril occurred, testator's wishes reduced to writing within 30-days of death, and limit of $500 worth of property devised)

    • Signed = personally or directed (D had to have been able to see signing)

- Subscribed = interested witness forfeits excess inheritance
- Applicable law:
    1. MO law
    2. Law at time and place of execution
    3. D's domicile at execution
    4. D's domicile at death

2. Mental State
    - Capacity
    - No insane delusions
    - No fraud
    - No undue influence
    - Knowledge of contents
    - Mistaken action, Not mistaken belief
    - If will partially invalid, then it is partially valid

3. Contents
    - Erroneous inclusion (curable), erroneous exclusion (incurable)
    - Incorporation by reference
        1. Pre-existing writing
        2. Referred to in will
        3. D intends to make it part of the will
        4. Document is adequately identified
    - Facts of independent significance
    - Written list for tangible property (signed, dated, referred to in will)
    - Interpretation of documents (can be overridden by express lang.)
        1. Relationship = normal

2. Estate conveyed:

—Life estate to A, remainder to A's heirs = just like its reads

• 120-hour survival = D can override this

LEGAL RESEARCH AND WRITING

The most important class you will take in law school is your first year legal research and writing class. Most law schools will have students do a legal memo and an appellate brief as part of this class using only the resource books in the school's law library, while forbidding students from using any computer-based legal research services. The reasoning behind not allowing 1L's to do computer-based legal research for their legal research and writing class is so they will learn to be proficient at using bound research materials, a skill that every lawyer should be proficient at, because many law firms try to hold down costs by limiting their computer-based legal research and sometimes using a reference book is easier and faster than computer-based legal research. Regardless of whether or not you agree with your law school's policy on limiting your computer-based legal research during your 1L days, the sooner you realize that legal research and writing is the most important class you will take in law school the better off you will be. Do not take your legal research and writing class lightly because the essence of being an effective lawyer is the ability to develop (i.e. research) and present a winning legal argument to the court. If there was ever a law school class you should strive to make top marks in, legal research and writing is that class.

New and better legal research methods are constantly being developed, and therefore; I am not going to attempt to provide you with a comprehensive guide to legal research, your legal research and writing professor has to get paid for something. I have, however, provided you with a list of basic research survival tips that should help you in your quest to become proficient at legal research and writing. Do not worry if you do not fully understand all of the survival tips at first, as you become more familiar with your law library and more comfortable doing legal research the survival tips will become more and more meaningful and helpful to you.

1. The librarian. Most 1L's don't have a clue where to begin when they step into a law library with their first legal research and writing assignment. Unfortunately, most 1L's overlook or just flat out ignore one of the most valuable resources in a law library, the librarian. The librarians in law libraries are typically highly educated professionals and experts at using the resources of their libraries. If you find yourself aimless walking around the law library unable to find the resource material you are looking for, stop your wondering and head straight for the librarian because he or she can probably help you locate the resource material you are searching for in a mater of seconds.

> **SIDEBAR:** If your legal research and writing class does not have a tour of your school's law library as part of the course's syllabus, make an effort to have the librarian take you on a guided tour of the library. A tour will get you familiar with the law library and save you time when it comes to finding resource materials. Also, if your law library has a printed guide to the library, take the time to pick one up, read through it, and keep it with you as a research tool.

2. The professor. Your legal research and writing professor is an expert in the field of legal research and writing. Do not be afraid to ask him or her questions about your research assignments or anything you do not understand about legal research and writing, whether it be how to properly cite a case or how to properly frame a legal argument. Law professors are there to teach you how to think and act like lawyers, make sure you don't let them off easy by being too afraid to take advantage of their knowledge.

> **SIDEBAR:** If you have a Teaching Assistant (TA) assigned to your legal research and writing class, don't let him or her off easy either. Most TA's are assigned to a legal research and writing class because they showed superior legal research and writing skills as 1L's. Use your TA as a resource to help you learn how to do legal research and writing, he or she is also there to help you.

> **SIDEBAR:** Don't be afraid to ask your legal research and writing professor for examples of your class assignments. Many professors keep examples of student assignments from past classes to use as examples in future classes. If your professor does not provide you with examples of your class assignments, do not be afraid to ask 2L's and 3L's who had your professor before for examples of your class assignments but always remember to adhere to your school's honor code when using any such examples. In other words, always do your own work. No plagiarizing please!

3. Get assignments done early. Make it a point to get every legal research and writing assignment done early. Your professor is no dummy and will be able to tell from your work whether or not you waited until the last minute to complete an assignment. Get your assignments done early so you have adequate time to check for grammatical, format, and citation errors. No use losing valuable points for mistakes that are preventable by simply doing an assignment early. Also, most professors have strict deadlines when it comes to turning in assignments and will not accept any work turned in after the deadline or will start taking points off by the minute after the deadline passes. Do not lose points by waiting until the last minute to do in one day an assignment you should have spent a week or more on.

4. Stay organized. Although you should stay organized in all your classes, when it comes to your legal research and writing class it is a must. Keep your assignments and research organized in such a manner that you can locate the materials you need without having to search through a pile of loose papers. Notebooks and dividers are cheap organizational tools but can be invaluable time saving tools if only used. A calendar that you can write the due dates of your assignments in is also a simple way to stay organized and on top of things. No surprises please when it comes to your legal research and writing class.

5. Learn how to use *The Bluebook*. *The Bluebook* is published by the Harvard Law Review and contains the uniform system of citation for legal materials. No law student can be without *The Bluebook* and it should be on your mandatory book purchase list. Become familiar with *The Bluebook*, take it with you when you go to the law library to do research, and use it when you write your legal papers. One of the most helpful things about *The Bluebook* is the fact that it lists all the abbreviations for legal materials by federal and state jurisdictions, which will help you know the name of the materials you are looking for and where to look for the materials in the law library.

6. Start with the law. Every time you begin a research project on a particular point or subject of the law, begin with the law itself. If you are dealing with a state law matter start with the state law and if you are dealing with a federal law matter start with the federal law. Most states refer to their laws as statutes, such as the Missouri Revised Statutes (RSMo). Federal laws are also referred to as statutes and are recorded in the *United States Code* (U.S.C.). For example, if I were asked to research a matter involving a client who was charged with stealing in Missouri, I would begin with the statute that deals with stealing in Missouri, namely, Section 570.030, RSMo. Once you have found the law or laws that you feel are involved in your research project, you have a starting point from which to begin looking for court cases and law review articles that interpret and analyze that law.

SIDEBAR: Being able to locate the law in your school's law library is a must, so be sure that you know where the federal and state statute materials are located. Due to the fact that you will be looking for court cases that explain the law and the courts' position(s) when it comes to interpreting and applying the law, I recommend using annotated statute books. Annotated statute books contain a list of cases that deal with each statute and can help to drastically reduce your research time. Annotated federal statutes can be found in the *United States Code Annotated* (U.S.C.A.). Annotated state statutes can be found in annotated materials for each state, such as *Vernon's Annotated Missouri Statutes* (Mo. Ann. Stat.). Annotated statute materials are materials that I find are actually quicker and easier to use than computer-based legal research services. Research smarter not harder.

SIDEBAR: Some resource materials sort legal cases and scholarly articles (i.e. law review articles) by subject. Some of these resources include *American Jurisprudence* (Am. Jur.) and *American Law Reports* (ALR). If I wanted an overview of contract law in America, I would look up the subject of "contracts" in these types of resource materials and review the list of cases and scholarly articles provided. When using such resources, remember that they will provide you an overview of cases from all the federal and state courts not just a particular state's courts, such as you would find in *Vernon's Annotated Missouri Statutes* (Mo. Ann. Stat.). Also, don't ignore the law review articles listed in these materials, as a good law review article will cite a lot of court cases on a particular subject, cases that you may want to cite in your own legal writings.

7. Find and read those cases. After you have compiled a list of cases, go find those cases and read them. It is easier to find cases when you know how cases are organized in bound resource materials. Court cases are organized in a series of books called reporters, each of which is listed in *The Bluebook*. For example, United States Supreme Court cases are listed in four reporters: *United States Reporter* (U.S.), *Supreme Court Reporter* (S. Ct.), *Lawyer's Edition* (L. Ed.), and *United States Law Week* (U.S.L.W.). By contrast, Missouri Supreme Court Cases are listed in only two reporters: *Missouri Reports* (Mo.) and *South Western Reporter* (S.W.). Learning where the different reporters are located in your school's law library will save a lot of time when it comes to finding the court cases you are looking for.

SIDEBAR: In order to find a case, you need to be able to understand what a case citation is telling you. This is easier than you think. All case citations follow the same format: case name, volume, reporter, page number, court, and date. Remember, this format is listed in *The Bluebook*. For example, using the citation of the *McCabe* case can help you learn how to find a case:

McCabe v. Director of Revenue, State of Missouri, 7 S.W.3d 12 (Mo.App. E.D. 1999).

McCabe v. Director of Revenue, State of Missouri = case name

7 S.W.3d 12 = volume 7 of the *South Western Reporter*, 3rd Edition, page 12

(Mo.App. ED 1999) = Missouri Court of Appeals - Eastern District, decided 1999

For another example, I will use a case cited in the *McCabe* case:

Reinert v. Director of Revenue, 894 S.W.2d 162, 164 (Mo. banc 1995)

Reinert v. Director of Revenue = case name

894 S.W.2d 162, 164 = volume 894 *South Western Reporter*, 2nd Edition, page 162 (starting page for the case), page 164 (specific page in the case that the citation came from).

(Mo. banc 1995) = Missouri Supreme Court sitting as full court (banc), decided 1995

SIDEBAR: When you are reading cases, be sure to pay attention to other cases cited in your cases because they may be cases that you want to use as well. Remember, the first case you read may end up simply being a resource for you to find other, more relevant cases that eventually find their way into your legal paper.

SIDEBAR: When you are reading cases, be sure to pay attention to any headnotes and/or footnotes that are present in the cases. The West publishing company publishes many of the reporters you will be using and places headnotes at the beginning of each case. These headnotes are typically a listing of the types of law covered in the case and can be a valuable research tool. Also, West has developed a classification system to use with its headnotes known as Keycites that organizes cases and legal materials by subject. Make sure your legal research and writing professor or TA shows you how to use the Keycite system. The LexisNexis computer-based legal research service also has a headnote classification system similar to West's that you should become familiar with when you start doing computer-based legal research. As for footnotes, always make it a point to read all of the footnotes in a case. The courts are found of hiding valuable information and case citations in footnotes.

SIDEBAR: When you find a court case in a reporter you think you will be using in your research, it is a good idea to print a copy of the case off at a photocopier machine and use the copy to work from. With a copy, you can highlight important portions of the case and other cases cited within the case itself. Never mark up a case in a reporter or tear one out of a reporter because your classmates are paying the same tuition you are and have the same right to use the law library's resource materials as you do. Also, damaging or destroying resource materials is typically a serious honor code violation.

8. **Shepardize each court case you cite to.** You want to be sure that every court case you cite to in a legal paper is still good law (i.e. the case has not been overturned by a later decision). To do this, you will need to Shepardize your cases. The act of Shepardizing simple means you have checked the appropriate volume of *Shepard's Acts and Cases by Popular Names* to determine whether or not a case is still good law. Each volume of Shepard's materials lists the complete history of the cases it contains and has a guide to explain the symbols Shepard's uses to let the reader know the status of a case. If your legal research and writing professor does not go over how to use Shepard's materials, make sure you request the he or she does or that you ask your TA or the librarian to show you how to use the materials.

9. Don't forget about constitutions and agency rules. When doing legal research on a subject do not forget to check if there are any provisions of the *United States Constitution* or a state's constitution that apply. Also, if you are dealing with an area of law that is administered by a federal or state agency, be sure to check if any agency rules or regulations apply to the matter you are researching. Federal agency rules can be found in the *Code of Federal Regulations* (C.F.R.). State agency rules can found in administrative compilations, such as the *Missouri Code of State Regulations Annotated* (Mo. Code Regs. Ann.).

10. Don't forget about secondary sources. Law review articles and treatises (books) on a law subject you are researching can be very helpful to you. Don't ignore citations to these sources when you come across them in your research. Remember these materials can be a source of court case listings that you can cite to in your legal papers. Also, citing to a law review article in a legal paper is a common practice for many lawyers.

11. Always check those pocket parts. Due to the fact that resource materials are expensive, most publishers update their materials on a yearly basis by issuing pocket parts. These pocket parts are placed in the back of a volume of material and contain the most up-to-date information on the material covered by that volume. For example, when this book was written the last hardbound edition of the Missouri Revised Statutes (RSMo) was published in 2000 but many statutes have been amended or revoked since 2000. Consequently, if I were researching a particular Missouri statute, I would always want to check the pocket part of the volume the statute was published in to see if the statute had been amended or revoked since 2000. Pocket parts are easy to forget about but, as many law students and lawyers alike have learned, this can be a very costly mistake to make.

12. Backup those files. Don't even attempt to create a legal paper without using a computer. Typewriters are relics of the past and it is time for you to leave them and the whiteout behind. I can't even imagine trying to format a legal paper on a typewriter, which I haven't touched since high school, after using a computer. Remember, however, that even though computers are wonderful things computers can malfunction, so be sure to backup your files on a floppy disk or CD no matter what. BACKUP YOUR FILES this is the golden rule of legal research and writing. There is nothing worse than having your computer erase your entire assignment as you are trying to print it out, just one hour before it is due. Protect yourself, BACKUP YOUR FILES.

13. Embrace and master computer-based legal research. There are two main competing computer-based legal research services in the legal community today, Westlaw and LexisNexis. When your law school allows you access to such services, take the time to learn how to use both of them proficiently. As a result of a dramatic drop in the cost of computer-based legal research services, many law firms and state and federal agencies are starting to get away from using hardbound reference materials in favor of such services. Learning to be proficient with both computer-based legal research services will make you a better researcher and a more highly sought after job applicant. Also, don't be afraid to embrace new research services when they come along. The world of technology will always be changing and computer-based legal research along with it.

SIDEBAR: Many law schools require their students to attend classes in the use of Westlaw and/or LexisNexis and provide them with instructional materials in the use of these services. I would advise you to keep these materials around for a quick reference guide because believe me you are not going to remember everything they tell you in your instructional classes.

SIDEBAR: I am partial to LexisNexis because I find it is easier to use then Westlaw but you will have to make up your own mind as to which service you prefer. One feature worth pointing out on LexisNexis is its Case Law Summaries, one of which appears at the top of each court case listed by the service. A Case Law Summary is a 1200 word or less summary of the case that also lists the legal authority relied on by the court in making its decision. Case Law Summaries can be a very useful research tool, as they may save you from having to read a case that is not going to be of any use to you. Case Law Summaries can also help you better understand a case, as well as help you better prepare for your classes.

14. Be sure to use all the resources available to you. Many law schools have a writing center to help students to properly prepare legal papers. If your law school has such a center use it, at least for help on completing your first legal paper. The center can help save you valuable grading points, as well as provide you with helpful tips on how to properly prepare a legal paper. Also, don't be afraid to use the campus undergraduate writing center for help on the general construction of a formal paper if your law school does not have a writing center. Remember, even published writers have editors.

15. Remember this list is not comprehensive. Remember this list of survival tips is not meant to be a comprehensive guide to legal research and writing but should be added to each time you learn something new about legal research and writing from your professors, TA's, and classmates, as well as from your own legal research and writing experiences.

LAW SCHOOL EXAMS

Law school exams are typically a combination of essay and multiple-choice questions covering all the material a professor has covered the entire semester. Although each law student will have to determine for themselves what method is most effective for him or her to use to study for a law school exam, the following list of survival tips should make preparing for a law school exam easier no matter what that determination turns out to be.

1. **Keep your class outlines up to date.** Due to the large amount of material covered by the typical law school exam, class outlines have emerged as the primary way law students prepare for exams. Consequently, each law student needs to keep his or her outlines up to date by working on them after class each day. Remember, creating an outline from your class notes as you go along during the semester will prevent you from having to waste valuable study time preparing outlines at the end of the semester.

2. **Make a summary sheet for each of your class outlines.** It is not unusual for a class outline to be well over 50-pages in length, and therefore; my advice to each law student is to make a summary sheet for each of your class outlines. An outline summary sheet should consist of only one piece of paper with information on the front and back. Take it from me, after reading through a 50+ pages outline you won't want to read anymore. An outline summary sheet can allow you to take a break from reading your entire outline, while you review only the major points contained in the outline. An outline summary sheet is also a good tool to use for some last minute studying before an exam. Better to study one sheet of paper when time is running short than 50+ pages. I have provided a sample of what an outline summary sheet should look like. The sample is a summary sheet that I actually used as a Hearing Officer for the Missouri Department of Revenue to remember the agency's rules, as well as losing and winning objections in Administrative Alcohol Hearings involving DWI's.

SIDEBAR: Many times when making an outline summary sheet you will find that you need to use a smaller than normal font. I have found that using a 10-point or 8-point font and organizing information in columns works best for getting large amounts of information onto one page.

SIDEBAR: For those of you who have been taking the time to read the Sidebars throughout this book, here's a bonus. There is also a summary sheet for this book included in this section, in addition to the summary sheet I used as a Hearing Officer. Use the summary sheet to remind you of the tips contained in this book.

3. Example of past exams. Some law professors will put examples of past exams on file in the law library or on the school's website for students to inspect. You need to be sure to inquire of your professors if they have put any of their old exams online or on file at the law library or have them available for your inspection by another method. Having an idea of what to expect on an upcoming exam is always a good idea.

4. Review sessions. If your professor holds a review session before an exam, go to it. Often times a professor will let students attending these sessions know what to expect on the exam. Also, don't be afraid to use these sessions as a vehicle to ask your professors to better explain an area of law you are having trouble understanding.

5. Make a study schedule. Make a study schedule that gives you plenty of time to prepare for each exam. Stick to your schedule and try to study in a place that is free of distractions. Remember, one of the best places to study is your school's law library.

6. Don't over study. Do not over study for an exam. Make sure you have breaks built into your study schedule. Learn to push yourself when you get tired but remember to give your brain a break every now and then.

7. Midterm exams. Many law schools have a midterm exam in at least one class during a student's first semester in law school. You should use the midterm as a practice run for your final semester exams. Find out what works for you and what doesn't when it comes to studying for an exam. Also, use the midterm exam to get a feel for what your professor's final exam will look like.

SIDEBAR: Don't panic if you do not do as well as you had hoped to on your midterm exams. A midterm exam won't make or break you as far as your final grade goes and some law schools don't even count them as part of your final grade. If you don't do well on your midterm exams, make an appointment to go over the exams with your professors and find out where you went wrong in your answers and ask them for suggestions on how to improve your performance.

---

8. Relax. The first thing you need to do when taking a law school exam is relax. Take a deep breath, tell yourself you have prepared for the exam and you know the material, exhale, and just relax. Law school is tough but don't make it tougher than it has to be by treating every exam like a life and death situation. You have a lot of exams to take, so just sit back and relax. Remember, a person can hinder his or her performance on an exam by worrying about the exam too much.

9. Read each question first. Before you answer a single question on a law school exam, read through each question first. By reading through each question on an exam, you can get an overall feel for the exam. Once you've read through all the questions, go back and answer the ones that you are sure you know the answers to first. This will give you confidence when it comes to the questions you are not quite sure you know what the answers should be.

10. Manage your time. Do not get hung up on one question, especially at the beginning of an exam. If you are having trouble with a question, skip it and come back to it. Better to miss one question you don't know the answer to then to miss five questions you do know the answers to simply because you ran out of time by wasting most of it on a single question. Be sure to know the time limits for each exam you take and plan your approach to the exam accordingly.

11. Essay questions. You do not have time to write an in-depth answer worthy of publication as part of a novel when it comes to law school exams. With essay questions, take a few moments to plan out your answer and then write a clear and concise one. The margins on an exam or a piece of scrap paper are excellent places to write an outline of your answer before writing it down for points. Don't be afraid to ask your professor if there is any particular form he prefers you to answer essay questions in. Also, answering essay questions in an outline type format with headings and subheadings is often a pretty good idea when one is crunched for time.

12. Multiple-choice questions. With multiple-choice questions you either know the material or you don't. Law professors are notorious for writing multiple-choice questions that have four or five very similar answers but only one right answer. Take your best shot and don't dwell on a single question for too long. If you are not sure about an answer to a multiple-choice question, mark what you think is the right choice, move on, and come back to the question if you have time to at the end of the test. Also, with multiple-choice questions try to eliminate the obviously wrong answers first, this usually reduces your choices to two answers giving you a 50/50 chance to answer the question right which is way better odds than 1 in 4 (25%) or 1 in 5 (20%).

> **SIDEBAR:** A good source for examples of the types of essay and multiple-choice questions that you are likely to encounter on a law school exam is the National Conference of Bar Examiners (NCBE) website at www.ncbex.org. The NCBE produces the essay and multiple-choice questions for state bar exams and periodically releases essay and multiple-choice questions from past bar exams to the public via their website. I strongly encourage you to visit the NCBE's website before your first law school exam. I have also provided an example essay question at the end of this section that I created based on the issues involved in a case I won on appeal.

> **SIDEBAR:** Aside from the NCBE's website, there are numerous books and study guides on the market today that provide examples of law school essay and multiple-choice questions, as well as tips and strategies for answering such questions. A visit to your campus or local bookstore or an online search for such materials should provide you with plenty of options to choose from. Aspen Publishers offers several books on essay and multiple-choice exams as part of their Emanuel Law Series available online at www.aspenpublishers.com.

13. Be wary of the take home exam. Sometimes a law professor will offer his or her students the choice between a take home exam or a regular exam, choose wisely. If I had it to do all over again, I would never vote for a take home exam. Take home exams are usually longer than a regular exam and are usually graded tougher by the professor. With take home exams there is very little room for error and many students find themselves spending 12 to 24 hours working on a take home exam instead of the 2 to 3 hours it would have taken them to complete a regular exam.

14. Don't be afraid to throw in the kitchen sink. Most essay questions on a law exam are issue-spotting exercises. Consequently, if you think there is an issue present in a question and you can support your answer, don't be afraid to address the issue in your answer. Some people call this approach the shotgun approach. Some of the worse advice I ever got from a law professor was to not use the shotgun approach on an essay exam. I followed this advice and my first year grades suffered. If you think it's an issue in the question then address it in your answer. Better to have the kitchen sink in your answer than to not even have a kitchen in it.

15. Open note and open book exams. Some law professors are found of giving open note and/or open book exams. You still need to study for these exams like they were regular closed book exams because you won't have time to read your notes (outlines) or law books when taking the exam to learn a concept you should have learned earlier in the semester. Your notes and books should be used as reference materials only, as a way to refresh your memory or confirm your answers. Organize your materials, such as putting thumb-tabs in your outlines and books, making a table of contents for your outlines, and making a summary sheet for each outline.

SIDEBAR: Instead of giving a traditional open note or open book exam, some law professors will allow students to bring in a 1-page sheet of information. If you have been making summary sheets for your outlines you will be ready for such an exam. If you haven't been making summary sheets for your outlines, the summary sheet format of organizing information into columns and using a smaller font (8 or 10-point) should help you get a lot of information onto a single sheet of paper. Once you have all the information on the summary sheet, make sure you know it before you take the exam because it is a reference tool not an excuse to not study for the exam.

16. Trouble remembering all that stuff? Try a worksheet or two. If you find that you are having trouble remembering lists and court cases for exams, try making some fill-in-the-blank worksheets out of your outlines by removing the lists and cases from your outlines and then going back and filling in the blanks as you study. The ability to cut and paste is yet another reason to have your outlines stored as electronic documents in a computer file. I used this technique myself as a 2L and 3L and found that after having written something down five or ten times I could remember it with relative ease. I just wish I would have thought to make study worksheets as a 1L, perhaps then my class ranking wouldn't have been so low after my first year. Also, when taking an exam that requires you to remember a lot of lists and cases, I always found it helpful to review the lists and cases right before the exam and then write the lists and cases down in the margins of the exam or on a piece of scratch paper (i.e. the blank pieces of paper you usually get with each exam to make notes on) as soon as I got the exam in my hands. I did this even before reading a single question on the exam. Most people have good short-term memories so make use of yours by using those exam margins and/or scratch paper wisely.

17. Flow charts. Aside from worksheets, flow charts or decision matrixes can also help you remember material for an exam. Try to limit your flow charts to one page per exam. Again, using a smaller font will prove helpful in getting a large amount of information into a flow chart or decision matrix.

18. Feeling overwhelmed. If you find yourself feeling overwhelmed by the prospect of taking a law school exam, do not be afraid to seek out help from counseling professionals. Many law schools have begun hiring stress counselors to help students cope with the rigors of law school. If your law school employs stress counselors, do not be afraid to go to them for help in dealing with your feelings of stress and anxiety. If your law school does not employ stress counselors, do not be afraid to seek out help from other counseling professionals located both on and off campus. Better to acknowledge your stress and do something to cope with it than to ignore it and let it build to an uncontrollable level.

19. Grades matter. If you need a little extra motivation to study remember that, contrary to popular belief, grades do matter in law school. The higher you finish in your law school class, the more job opportunities are going to come your way. Study hard and study smart.

SIDEBAR: If you are still in need of extra motivation to get good grades in law school, the following is an actual employment advertisement placed by a well-known firm in Kansas City, Missouri. Please notice the firm's emphasis on academic excellence:

Shook, Hardy & Bacon's ERISA Litigation Section, located in suburban Kansas City on the Kansas side, is expanding. The Section must add another litigation associate. The new attorney must have at least two years experience in complex litigation, some of which must be in ERISA. Exceptional oral and written communications skills will be required, as will the ability to work in a multiple project, fast-paced, rapidly changing and intellectually challenging environment. The Firm's unusually high academic requirements must be met; therefore, please submit a law school transcript along with a resume.

Unfortunately, although I can author a book on how to succeed in law school, as well as legal essays, journal articles, agency rules, and winning motions and appellate briefs, my class ranking in law school would make it very difficult for me to land a job with the above firm. The validity of a system that denies lawyers opportunities because of their law school grades is debatable but the sooner you learn that it is the system that you will be competing in for legal jobs the sooner you will come to the realization that getting good grades in law school is extremely important.

Sample Of Outline Summary Sheet

Hearing Procedures – 12 CSR 10-24.030 & 302.505 RSMo (Supp. 2002); 302.530 RSMo (2000):

1. **Written request** must be made within 15-days of notice being issued in person or within 18-days if notice issued by mail – 12 CSR 10.24.030(1); §302.530.1 RSMo (2000)
   - --Request must **specify** whether driver wants **telephonic or in person hearing** §302.530.3
   - **--Telephonic hearing is default remedy** if hearing type not specified by driver
   - --If delivered by **United States mail, after date of suspension/revocation start date, postmark** stamped on envelope is **deemed to be the filing date** of request
   - --Request must be sent to: **Missouri Department of Revenue, Drivers and Vehicle Services Bureau, P.O. Box 3700, Jefferson City, Missouri 65105-3700**
   - **--Temporary privileges** issued upon timely request, effective until date of final order §302.530.2
2. **Failure to surrender** valid Missouri license at time notice is issued results in waiver of hearing – 12 CSR 10.24.030(2)
   - 2(a)--If driver's Missouri license is lost, destroyed, or stolen and **driver is not currently suspended or revoked,** he must apply for duplicate license** and surrender the 60-day driving receipt with hearing request
   - 2(b)--If driver's Missouri license is lost, destroyed, or stolen and **driver is currently suspended or revoked, driver must submit a notarized affidavit** to that effect with the hearing request.
3. **Failure to properly request hearing** will result in a **waiver** of a hearing. 12 CSR 10.24.030(3).
4. **Continuance** for good cause must be filed no later than 6-days prior to hearing date. 12 CSR 10.24.030(4)
   - **--Only one (1) continuance**
   - **--Good Cause =** death, unavailability, or incapacitating illness (written statement from doctor required)
5. **Delay in a hearing without good cause** shall not stay suspension/revocation. 12 CSR 10.24.030(5)
6. **Party may be represented by an attorney** – 12 CSR 10.24.030(6); §302.530.3
   - **--Notice** to be sent to party and attorney of record (if known at time of notice)
   - **--Suspension/revocation stayed** until final order is issued by hearing office §302.530.2
   - **--Hearing conducted by Department of Revenue Examiners** §302.530.3
   - **--Examiners must be licensed to practice law** §302.530.3
7. **Issues at hearing** – 12 CSR 10-24.030(7) & §302.505.1; §302.530.4:
   - **21 and over or minor arrested for DWI (.08% or higher)**
     1. **Probable cause** to believe driver was driving with BAC in of .08% or higher
     2. **Valid test** shows BAC of .08% or higher
   - **Zero Tolerance – .02% - .079%**
     1. **Probable cause to stop:**
        - --traffic violation
        - --reasonable suspicion that driver was drunk (i.e. driver suspected of DWI)
        - --reasonable suspicion that driver was driving with BAC of .02% or higher
     2. **Valid Test** shows BAC of .02% - .079%
8. **Hearing conducted in accordance with Chapter 536 RSMo** - §302.530.5
9. **Final decision** shall be rendered subsequent to hearing – 12 CSR 10.24.030(8) & 302.530.6
   - --Stating **findings of fact** and **conclusions of law**
   - **--Party** shall be mailed copy of decision by **certified mail**
   - **--Attorney** shall be mailed copy of decision by **regular mail**
   - **--Decision final** unless appealed de novo within **15-days from date certified letter** 12 CSR 10-34.030 (11)
10. **Party may present evidence** at hearing showing BAC not above .08% when driving - 12 CSR 10-24.030(9)
    - **--May subpoena witnesses** in accordance with procedures of §536.077 RSMo (2000)
    - **--Subpoena witnesses by requesting** subpoena from DOR at least **5 working days prior** to hearing
    - **--If subpoenaed witness does not appear,** hearing will be **continued for DOR to enforce subpoena** in accordance with §536.077
    - **--If witness dead,** may consider written testimony prepared **at or near time of incident**
    - **--Party may object** to written testimony of dead witnesses
11. **Party may examine** all available evidence **before hearing** – 12 CSR 10-24.030(10)
    - **--Any witness may be cross-examined** during the hearing
12. **Director may adopt rules to enforce §** 302.530 – 302.530.8

Front Of Sheet

Losing Objections

AIR Not Sworn Report (Notary)
--AIR signed before notary = sworn report (even if AIR sent back to trooper by DOR to fix discrepancy in signature dates)
Cessor v. DOR, 71 S.W.3d 217 (Mo. App. W.D. 2002)

BAC Results Obtained Over 1-Hour After Arrest
--Legislature anticipated times when such delays would occur
Green v. DOR, 961 S.W.2d 936 (Mo. App. E.D. 1998)
Cox v. DOR, 756 S.W.2d 943 (Mo. App. S.D. 1988)

BAC Results Within Margin Of Error
--BAC results .08%+ but within margin of error of breathalyzer and/or testing solution are valid
State ex rel DOR, 997 S.W.2d 121 (Mo. App. S.D. 1999)
Lewis v. Lohman, 936 S.W.2d 582 (Mo. App. W.D. 1996)

Belching During 15-minute Observation/Breath Test
--Belching does not violate DOH regulations
Daniels v. DOR, 977 S.W.3d 42 (Mo. App. S.D. 2001)

Breathalyzer Only Tested At .04% And Not .08%
--DOH regs allow testing at .04% and/or .01%
19 CSR 25-30.031(7)

Breathalyzer Printout Not In Admin Packet
--Can prove BAC using AIR -- printout not needed
Grace v. DOR, 77 S.W.3d 29 (Mo. App. E.D. 2002)
Chevalier v. DOR, 928 S.W.2d 388 (Mo. App. W.D. 1996)

Certificate of Analysis Not Present In Packet
--Certificate of Analysis no longer required by DOH Regs.
Sheridan v. DOR, 103 S.W.3d 878 (Mo. App. E.D. 2003)

Certificate Analysis Lot # Different Than Maint. Report
--Not fatal flaw if lot # on Maintenance Report is different from COA b/c COA only has to list solution/manufacturer
Milligan v. DOR, 78 S.W.2d 215 (Mo. App. W.D. 2002)

Citation Not In Arrest Packet
--Copy of complaint and/or citation not required
Bennett v. DOR, 705 SW2d 118 (Mo. App. W.D. 1986)

Confrontation Clause:
--Protection of C. Clause does not apply (civil proceeding)
Krieg v. DOR, 39 S.W.3d 574 (Mo. App. E.D. 2001)

Dentures In During Testing
--Dentures in do not violate DOH regs.
Green v. DOR, 961 S.W.2d 936 (Mo. App. E.D. 1998)
Farr v. DOR, 914 S.W.2d 38 (Mo. App. S.D. 1996)

Double Jeopardy:
--Suspension of driving privileges not punishment
State v. Mayo, 915 S.W.2d 758 (Mo. Sup. 1996)

Due Process -- Arbitrary & Capricious
--§302.505 details standards and penalty for drunk driving
Vetter v. King, 692 S.W.2d 255 (Mo. Sup. 1995)

Due Process -- Dual Role of Hearing Officer:
--De novo review sufficient safeguard to ensure due process where hearing officer both prosecutes and represents DOR
Bradley v. McNeil, 709 S.W.2d 153 (Mo. App. E.D. 1986)
Dove v. DOR, 704 S.W. 2d 713 (Mo. App. W.D. 713)

Hearsay -- Admin Packet Contains Hearsay Statements
--Admin Packet admissible under hearsay exceptions (i.e. 302.312 and business record exception 490.692)

Illegal Arrest Of Driver -- Officer Lacked Jurisdiction
--Illegal arrest not relevant - No Exclusionary Rule
Barish v. DOR, 872 S.W.2d 167 (Mo. App. W.D. 1994)
Kimber v. DOR, 817 S.W.2d 627 (Mo. App. W.D. 1991)

Implied Consent Defective But Valid BAC Results
--Compliance with §577.041.1 not required to admit results
Crabtree v. DOR, 65 S.W.3d 557 (Mo. App. W.D. 2002)

Miranda Warnings Not Given
--Irrelevant if Miranda given because no Exclusionary Rule
Tebow v. DOR, 921 S.W.2d 110 (Mo. App. W.D. 1996)

No Operation -- Corpus Delicti Rule
--Corpus Delicti Rule does not apply to admin. proceedings, admissions of driving OK to show officer had probable cause
Webb v. DOR, 896 S.W.2d 517 (Mo. App. W.D. 1995)
Tuggle v. DOR, 727 S.W.2d 168 (Mo. App. W.D. 1987)

No Operation -- Engine Running But Car In Park
--Asleep/unconscious with engine running = operation
Cox v. DOR, 98 S.W.3d 548 (Mo. Sup. 2003)

No Operation -- Office Did Not See Driver Driving
--Circumstantial evidence can be used to establish driving
Molthan v. DOR, 32 S.W.3d 643 (Mo. App. W.D. 2000)
Delzell v. Lohman, 983 S.W.2d 633 (Mo. App. S.D. 1999)
Rogers v. DOR, 947 S.W.2d 475 (Mo. App. E.D. 1997)

No Printouts Attached To Maintenance Report
--Better that printouts be attached but not required to be
Sheridan v. DOR, 103 S.W.3d 878 (Mo. App. E.D. 2003)
Smith v. DOR, 948 S.W.2d 219 (Mo. App. E.D. 1997)

No Probable Cause For Initial Stop (Driver 21+)
--Probable cause to stop is not an issue in Admin. Hearings
Riche v. DOR, 987 S.W.2d 331 (Mo. Sup. 1999)

No Probable Cause To Arrest Because No FST's Done
--Can develop probable cause without FST's
Brown v. DOR, 85 S.W.3d 1 (Mo. Sup. 2002)

No Probable Cause To Arrest -- Witness Statements Only
--Can develop probable cause on witness statements only
Parres v. DOR, 75 S.W.2d 311 (Mo. App. E.D. 2002)
Rain v. DOR, 46 S.W.3d 584 (Mo. App. E.D. 2001)

No Probable Cause To Stop Minor Having BAC .08%+
--Do not have to show P/C to stop minor charged with DWI
Baldwin v. DOR, 38 S.W.3d 401 (Mo. Sup. 2001)

15-minute - Driver Not Observed Entire Time
--15 minute observation satisfied where driver not observed entire time and no testimony of oral intake or vomiting
Daniels v. DOR, 48 S.W.3d 42 (Mo. App. S.D. 2001)
Holley v. Lohman, 977 S.W.2d 310 (Mo. App. S.D. 1998)

--15 minute observation can be done by arresting officer and can begin at initial contact
Hollingshead v. DOR, 36 S.W.3d 443 (Mo. App. E.D. 2001)

Some Winning Objections
1. AIR not properly signed and/or notarized
2. Blood Test given using an alcohol-based swab
3. Certification Section not filled out by testing officer
4. Check List not filled out by testing officer
5. DOH permits expired before testing/maintenance done

Back of Sheet

ULTIMATE SURVIVAL GUIDE SUMMARY SHEET

PART I: SURVIVAL TIPS FOR 1L's

INTRODUCTION: WHY DID I WRITE IT
Wrote book to help law students succeed.

BEST TIP
BAR/BRI outlines – best outlines available

BEFORE STARTING LAW SCHOOL
--Law school is a 50-70 hours per week job
--Takes some time off before starting law school
--Move to law school town early
--Being a law student is your job

THE LAW SCHOOL ENVIRONMENT
--Law professors:
    --Deserve your respect
    --Show respect by coming to class
    --Get to class on time
    --Don't judge a professor based on 1st day
--Law school staff:
    --Deserve to be treated as equals
    --Are there to help law students
    --Get to know them - they can help you
    --Run the day-to-day operations of school
--Law school students:
    --Come from all walks of life
    --All are under stress like you
    --Get to know them - they can help you
    --Valuable resource

THE LAW SCHOOL ROUTINE
1. Go to orientation = good information there
2. Know your title & place = 1L, 2L, 3L
3. Know what to learn = to think like a lawyer
4. Student handbook = get it, read it
5. Honor code = know it, follow it
6. Use your mentor = gain knowledge
7. Check for first-day-of-class assignments
8. Law books = expensive, good to make notes in
9. Go to class = can get bonus points for going
10. Take good notes = they make good outlines
11. Keep outlines up to date = saves study time
12. Make a study schedule = stick to schedule
13. Come prepared for class = know the cases
14. Don't be afraid to raise hand = ask questions
15. Get to know classmates = they can help you
16. Take a class in every bar subject = it helps
17. Get organized and stay organized
18. Save every piece of paper = put in a shoebox
19. Embrace technology = have computer skills
20. Keep up with law community = get involved
21. Stay focused and stay positive

22. Things can walk off = stuff can get stolen
23. Remember all that money has to be paid back
24. Write down your goals for law school
25. Do forget about outside world = read the paper
26. Don't make a stupid mistake = no convictions

CASE BRIEFS
--Formal briefs no more than 1 to 2 pages in length
--Formal briefs take longer to produce
--Easier to brief cases in the margins of law books

CLASS OUTLINES
1. Commercial outlines are worth the money
2. Keep your outlines up to date
3. Keep an eye out for guy or gal with old outlines
4. Lists from professors put in outlines
5. Do not try to understand the example outline

LEGAL RESEARCH AND WRITING
--Most important class in law school
1. The librarian = ask him or her for help
2. Professor = make sure he/she explains things
3. Get assignments done early = no silly mistakes
4. Stay organized = no loose papers
5. Learn to use The Bluebook = uniform citation
6. Start all research projects with the law
7. Find/read those cases = use to find other cases
8. Shepardize each case = no overturned cases
9. Don't forget about constitutions & agency rules
10. Don't forget secondary sources = law journals
11. Always check pocket parts = in back of books
12. Backup those files = floppy disk or CD
13. Embrace and master computer-based research
14. Be sure to use all the resources available
15. Remember this list is not comprehensive

LAW SCHOOL EXAMS
1. Keep up with class outlines = saves study time
2. Make summary sheets = last minute reviews
3. Examples of past exams = ask if available
4. Review sessions = attend and ask questions
5. Make a study schedule = enough time to prepare
6. Don't over study = schedule study breaks
7. Midterm exams = learn from your mistakes
8. Relax = plenty of exams ahead of you - relax
9. Read each question first = get a feel for exam
10. Manage time = don't waste time on one "?"
11. Essay questions = issue spotters
12. Multiple-choice = eliminate wrong choices
13. Be wary of take home exams = usually harder
14. Don't be afraid to throw in the kitchen sink
15. Open note/open book exams = organize notes
16. Trouble remembering lists = worksheets
17. Flow charts = help in remembering
18. Feeling overwhelmed = seek help
19. Grades matter = higher rank = more job offers

Front of Sheet

MAINTAINING YOUR PERSPECTIVE
1. Schedule some time off
2. Not everybody can be in the top 10%
3. Law school doesn't always make sense
4. You're not the only one who hated law school
5. Speaking of waiting = wait to get married

PART II: SURVIVAL TIPS FOR 2L's

SURVIVAL TIPS FOR 2L's
1. Spend some time self-evaluating
2. Stay focused = remember law school is 3 years
3. Specializing = areas of the law that interest you
4. Your job search starts now!

PART III: SURVIVAL TIPS FOR 3L's AND NEW LAWYERS

THE BAR EXAM
1. It's all about the bar exam = no pass, no job
2. Take a class in every bar exam subject
3. Don't forget about the MPRE
4. Save a copy of your bar exam application
5. Sign up for a bar exam review course
6. Review survival tips for law school exams
7. Concentrate on one bar exam at a time
8. Don't make a stupid mistake in law school
9. It's not the end of the world

FINDING THAT FIRST LAW JOB
1. Do not wait to start your job search
2. Get to know the career development office staff
3. Fill that resume
    A. Clubs, societies, and organizations
    B. Internships and clerkships
    C. Teaching and research assistant
    D. Competitions
    E. Get something published
    F. Study abroad
    G. Duel Degree Programs
    H. Certificate of emphasis
    I. Volunteering
    J. Grades
4. Go to on-campus interviews
5. Internship/clerkship with employer you like
6. Network
7. Start putting together a wardrobe
8. Keep your resume updated
9. Websites
10. Watch those deadlines

KEEPING THAT FIRST REAL LAW JOB
1. You don't know it all = learn from other lawyers
2. Develop a good professional reputation
3. Watch out for employment contracts

4. Don't burn bridges
5. Keep networking
6. Watch those finances
7. Maintain your perspective
8. Don't forget about job finding survival tips

EPIGLOGUE
Keep adding to this book and you will be adding to your knowledge.

Notes:

Back of Sheet

Example Essay Question

At 1:30 a.m., Deputy Sheriff Scott Doright ("Deputy Doright") stopped a car driven by Janet Dowrong ("Janet") for failing to have a valid license plate. While approaching Janet's car on foot, Deputy Doright noticed that Janet did have a valid temporary license plate displayed in the back window of the car, in compliance with Missouri law. After seeing the valid temporary license plate, Deputy Doright asked Janet for her license and vehicle registration and then asked Janet to exit her car and have seat in the back of his patrol car. Janet complied with Deputy Doright's requests and took a seat in the patrol car. While Deputy Doright waited for the results of a computer check of Janet's license and registration, he questioned Janet about her activities that night and wanted to know what she was doing out so late. Janet informed Deputy Doright that she and her boyfriend Matt had been at a local bar for most of the night and when the bar closed that she and Matt had agreed to give Gina and Mark a ride home. Janet then informed Deputy Doright that the passengers in her car were Matt, Mark, and Gina. At this point in the conversation, Deputy Doright asked Janet if she had any illegal drugs or contraband in the car, to which Janet replied that she did not. Deputy Doright then asked Janet if she objected to him searching her car, to which Janet replied that she did not. Deputy Doright then ordered Matt, Mark, and Gina out of the car and performed a thorough search of the car. During the search, Deputy Doright found a homemade pipe containing burnt marijuana residue. Janet was arrested for possession of less than 35 grams of marijuana and possession of drug paraphernalia, both misdemeanor offenses in Missouri.

(1) At trial, Janet's attorney files a motion to suppress all evidence against her on the grounds that Officer Doright illegally detained Janet after he noticed the temporary license plate lawfully displayed in the car's rear window. During a hearing on the motion, Officer Doright testifies that the reason for his stop of Janet's car was satisfied when he saw the temporary license plate, that he never asked her about the temporary license plate during the stop, and that he had no reason to suspect Janet had anything illegal in her car when he asked to search it. Should the trial court grant or deny Janet's motion to suppress?

(2) If the trial court does not grant Janet's motion to suppress, is there enough evidence to convict her of possession of marijuana?

Example Answers To Essay Question

(1) The purpose of the Fourth Amendment is to prevent unreasonable search and seizures. The Supreme Court has declared the Fourth Amendment's protections against unreasonable search and seizures enforceable against the states through the Due Process Clause of the Fourteenth Amendment. Article I, Section 15 of the *Missouri Constitution* is co-extensive with the Fourth Amendment in its protection against unreasonable search and seizures. In *Deleware v. Prouse*, the Supreme Court determined that the stopping of an automobile and its occupants constitutes a seizure under the Fourth and Fourteenth Amendments. Missouri courts have found that if a traffic stop of a motorist extends beyond the time reasonably necessary to investigate the purpose of the initial stop without the development of new reasonable suspicion to detain the driver further the traffic stop may lose its lawful character. Due to the fact that Officer Doright testified that his initial purpose for stopping Janet's car was satisfied when he saw the temporary license plate in the car's back window and that he had no reason to believe that Janet had anything illegal in her car when he asked to search it, unless the trial court finds that it was reasonable for Deputy Doright to detain Janet after he saw the temporary license plate, the trial court should grant Janet's motion to suppress.

(2) Presently in Missouri law, there is a split in the courts with regard to whether or not burnt residue is sufficient to support a conviction for possession of an illegal substance. As only burnt residue was found in the homemade pipe seized from Janet's car, the question of whether there is sufficient evidence to convict Janet of possession of marijuana will depend on the trial court's position with regard to residue. If the trial court supports the position that residue is enough to convict for possession of an illegal substance, there is enough evidence to convict Janet of possession of marijuana. If the trial court does not support the position that residue is enough to support a conviction for possession of an illegal substance, there is not enough evidence to convict Janet of possession of marijuana.

SIDEBAR: Try to be clear and concise in your answers, while exploring all the possibilities presented by the fact pattern contained in the question. Remember that you will typically not have enough time to write a long, drawn out answer worthy of publication and should try to get to the point in your answers in as few words as possible. The example answer to question two (2) is an excellent example of how the best answer to a law school exam question just might be "maybe."

SIDEBAR: When writing an answer to an essay question, it is always a good idea to list the names of the important cases on which the law that you are basing your answer was founded. Word of caution, however, when listing a case in your answer make sure that it is the correct case and that you know the correct spelling of the names of the parties involved in the case.

MAINTAINING YOUR PERSPECTIVE

Every year seems to bring with it a news story or newspaper article detailing the suicide of a law school student that felt he or she couldn't handle the pressures of law school anymore. Don't ever let yourself think that success in law school is worth killing yourself over. Law school is supposed to be a celebration of higher-level learning, not a life and death ordeal. The following survival tips are meant to help you keep law school in perspective and to deal with the constant pressures you will find yourself under as a law student.

1. Schedule some time off. Time away from your law school studies is essential to maintaining a good mental outlook on life. If at all possible, try to keep your 50–70 hours per week of law school studies confined to Monday through Friday by coming in early and staying late. Reserve the weekends for yourself and your family. This is especially important for married and non-traditional students supporting families to try to do. Get away from the law school, go to the park, take in a movie, or go to an athletic event. Just do something besides studying law. Now, I know that you may not be able to avoid the law school every weekend but try to have at least one day a week that you don't do any studying or worrying about law school.

2. Not everybody can be in the top 10%. Not every law student can finish in the top 10% of his or her class. Do the best you can and let the chips fall where they may. There are plenty of law jobs waiting for you out there. A recent survey showed that while 40,000 students graduated from law school each year, 40,000 lawyers left the legal profession each year. If your grades aren't as high as you want them to be keep trying and also keep adding to your resume by involving yourself in extracurricular activities that don't involve grades.

SIDEBAR: For those of you needing extra comfort when it comes to grades, my first semester grades in law school averaged out to be 70.5%, good enough for a place near the bottom of my class and less than a percentage point away from being placed on academic probation. I kept trying, however, and was able to raise my overall average to near 80% before I graduated and moved up in class rank by nearly 100 spots. Don't be surprised if several of your law professors have similar stories.

3. Law school doesn't always make sense. Nobody ever understands everything that goes on in law school so don't sweat the things that are beyond your control. Case in point, as a 3L, I turned in a paper for my negotiation class and entered the same paper in a national writing contest. I got a 68% on the paper but won the contest and received $1,000 and a free trip to San Francisco, California. Go figure.

4. You're not the only person who ever hated law school. If you find yourself hating law school after your first semester or year, take some time to think about whether you really want to be a lawyer or not. Don't let hating law school keep you from becoming a lawyer if that is what you really think you want to do with your life. Many lawyers hated law school but love being lawyers; I am one of those lawyers. I hated law school but always knew I wanted to be a lawyer because of a lawyer's unique ability to help people. It is better to come to the conclusion sooner rather than later that you do not want to be a lawyer because paying for one semester or year worth of law school is a lot cheaper than paying for 3 years worth of law school. Do not rush into any decision to quit law school but take the time to think it through. Remember, many a lawyer hated law school but loved being a lawyer. Sometimes a rough journey is worth the reward waiting at the end of that journey.

5. Speaking of waiting. For those of you who are considering getting married while you are in law school, my simple advice is don't. The first year of marriage is stressful enough getting to know the real person you married and you do not want to add the stress of law school to the stress that comes with a new husband or wife. If you are planning on getting married, get married at least a year before you start law school or make it a post bar exam results affair because you need that first year of marriage to be one in which you are focused mainly on your marriage and not your law studies. Couples in love, considered yourselves has having been warned.

SIDEBAR: Another piece of advice that married couples or couples looking to get married should adhere to is that only one person should be in school at any given time. Trying to make a marriage or relationship work when both people are in school is an uphill road at best. Take if from me, my wife and I were both in school at the same time, she pursuing an undergraduate degree in Art Education and me chasing that elusive JD, and it was no picnic around our house. Too many homework assignments, papers, and tuition bills for our taste and mental well being.

PART II: 2L'S

SURIVIVAL TIPS FOR THE SECOND YEAR LAW STUDENT

FOR 2L'S

There is an old saying about law school that goes something like this, "in the first year they scare you to death, in the second year they read you to death, and in the third year they bore you death." Like other sayings about law school, the validity of this saying is debatable, as I sure remember reading a lot in my first and third years of law school just like I did in my second year. I also remember being just as scared of failure in my second and third years of law school as I was in my first year. For me, as well as for the majority of lawyers I spoke with while writing this book, the second year of law school is affectionately referred to as the "forgotten year" of law school. Unlike the first year of law school when everything is new and fresh and the third year when the excitement of graduation fills the air, the second year of law school if filled with the monotony of routine and, in law school, routine means reading lots and lots of court cases. The following survival tips are meant to help 2L's deal with the monotony of their second year of law school and stay focused on their goal of succeeding in law school. For those of you who will be happy to learn that this is the smallest section in the book, you are welcome. For those of you who find yourselves wondering why this is smallest section in the book, I ask that you please reserve your judgment until after you have experienced the "forgotten year" of law school firsthand.

1. **Spend some time self-evaluating.** Before you begin your life as a 2L, take some time to evaluate your first year in law school and where you stand going into your second year. If you did not do as well as you had hoped to do during your first year, take some time to analyze what study or test taking strategies worked for you and what strategies did not then write out a plan detailing what steps you are going to take to improve your performance in law school. Also, the beginning of the second year of law school is perhaps the last time that it would be a realistic and financially beneficial option to quite law school if you have come to the decision, after taking the time to seriously evaluate yourself, your future, and your goals, that being a lawyer is not for you.

SIDEBAR: If you are having trouble coming up with a plan to improve your law school performance, do not be afraid to approach your law school professors, counselors, and classmates for advice on how to improve your performance. Sometimes the biggest obstacle to coming up with a solution to a problem is not in admitting that you have a problem but in admitting that you need help in finding the solution to the problem.

SIDEBAR: If you still haven't decided if you want to become a lawyer or not, Niche Press, LLC, offers a series of books called DecisionBooks® centered around career choices in the law, such as *What Can You Do With A Law Degree* and *Should You Really Be a Lawyer? The Guide to Smart Career Choices Before, During & After Law School,* that might prove helpful to you. More information about DecisionBooks can be found at www.decisionbooks.com.

---

2. Stay focused. When the routine of a 2L sets in, you will find it more and more difficult to say focused on your law school studies. Do whatever you have to do to keep your focus because a lack of focus in your second year can result in lower grades and a significant drop in your class ranking that you may not be able to recover from during your third year of law school. My best advice to you about staying focused is to take the time to review the survival tips I have provided for 1L's in Part I of this book before the start of classes your second year, especially if you did not take law classes during the summer between your first and second year, as reviewing the tips will help to get you refocused on succeeding in law school. Also, it is more important than ever to get and stay organized during the second year of law school, as staying organized will help you stay on top of your reading assignments, which do, at least in theory, increase during the second year of law school. Getting and staying organized will also help you to stay focused on your main goal as a law student, namely, achieving success in law school.

3. Specializing. During the second and third years of law school, most schools allow their students more freedom when it comes to choosing which classes to take. If you found you enjoyed a particular area of the law during your first year, you might want to consider taking other classes in that area or earning a certificate of emphasis in that area if your law school offers such certificates. Before deciding to specialize in an area of law, however, you might want to take the time to talk to an employment counselor, law professor, or a lawyer practicing in the particular area you are interested in about the advantages and disadvantages of specializing in that area, as well as review the survival tips I offer to 3L's about certificates of emphasis and to 1L's about taking a class in every subject covered on the bar exam.

> **SIDEBAR:** If you decide to specialize in a specific area of law, do not forget about the graduation requirements that most law schools have with regard to required courses that must be completed before a student will be eligible to graduate, as you do not want to be the student who earns of certificate of emphasis but not a law degree.

> **SIDEBAR:** Survival tips about certificates of emphasis can be found in Part III under the heading **Finding That First Law Job**. Survival tips about taking a class in every subject on the bar exam can be found in Part I under the heading **The Law School Routine**.

4. Your job search starts now! If you took my advice in the **Introduction** section of this book, then you took the time to read through the entire book and know that your job search for your first real law job started as soon as you stepped foot into your law school. If you did not heed my advice in the **Introduction** section, I earnestly and sincerely recommend that you immediately turn to Part III of the book and read my survival tips for finding that first law job because time is running out for you to find a legal job that will prove both satisfying and rewarding to you.

> **SIDEBAR:** For those of you who heeded my advice in the **Introduction** section of this book, kudos to you, as you are well on your way to finding your first real law job. You have also come to understand that important information can be found in every section and on every page of this book, information that can help you throughout your journey from law student to new lawyer.

PART III: 3L'S AND NEW LAWYERS

SURVIVAL TIPS FOR THE THIRD YEAR LAW STUDENT AND NEW LAWYER

THE BAR EXAM

Most states require that law school graduates take and pass the state's bar exam before they can be licensed to practiced law in the state. A state's bar exam typically consists of four parts: (1) Multistate Essay Exam (MEE), comprised of essay questions, (2) Multistate Bar Exam (MBE), comprised of 200 multiple choice questions, (3) Multi State Performance Test (MPT), a practical exercise using instructions and materials provided to solve a legal problem, and (4) Multistate Professional Responsibility Exam (MPRE), comprised of 50 multiple-choice questions about professional responsibility. The MEE, MBE, and MPT are usually taken together over a two or three day period and is the combination of tests that makes up what is traditionally known as the bar exam. The MPRE is typically given separately and most states allow a person to take the MPRE prior to or after sitting for the bar exam. The following survival tips are not meant to be a complete guide to passing a bar exam but are designed to help law students to have an idea of what is waiting for them after law school and how to better prepare for one of the most important tests of their lives.

1. **It's all about the bar exam.** Your 3 years in law school is leading up to one final moment of truth, the bar exam. For most law school graduates, to practice law you have to pass the bar exam. Many employers will refuse to hire new law graduates before they pass the bar exam or will condition their continued employment on receiving a passing score on the bar exam. It's all about the bar exam. Finishing in the top 10% of your law school class won't help you very much if you cannot pass the bar exam. Don't let your law school vision be shortsighted, keep your focus on the bar exam throughout your law school career and take the steps necessary to prepare yourself for the exam.

2. **Take a class in every subject covered on the bar exam.** It is a popular practice in law school to advise students that they do not have to take a class in every subject that is on a state's bar exam to pass the exam. This is true but, having learned the hard way how difficult it is to study for a bar exam subject that I didn't have a class on, I would advise all law students to defy conventional wisdom and take a class in every subject on the bar exam. Take it from me, it is a lot easier to study for a bar exam subject once you have had a class on it. If you noticed that I gave this exact same

tip in an earlier section then it should serve to reinforce how important I think it is that you follow this advice.

> **SIDEBAR:** Your law school should be able to provide you with a list of subjects that are covered on a state's bar exam, if not, a visit to that state's government or courts web pages should be able to provide you with bar exam information. Also, the BAR/BRI web page at www.barbri.com routinely lists each state's bar exam subjects.

3. Don't forget about the MPRE. If you are taking the bar exam in a state that requires the MPRE, make sure you do not forget about this part of the bar exam. Remember, it is usually given separate from the other parts of the bar exam. Find out what your state's requirements are for the MPRE and take this part of the bar exam as early as possible. For example, Missouri allows a person sitting for the bar exam to take the MPRE up to 3 years before the exam or within one year following the exam, however, a person passing the bar exam cannot be licensed until he or she has also passed the MPRE portion of the exam. Ideally, you want to take the MPRE during your second year in law school after you have had a class in professional responsibility. Taking the MPRE your second year will give you one less thing to worry about when the bar exam rolls around at the end of your third year, as well as give you plenty of time to retake the MPRE if you don't pass it the first time around.

> **SIDEBAR:** Without fail, a few students from each law class forget about the MPRE and fail to take it before sitting for the bar exam and end up passing the bar exam but not being able to receive their law licenses because they do not have a MPRE score on file with the state. These students are forced to wait for the next available MPRE test session and for their scores to be forwarded to the state before becoming eligible for a law license, which can result in a delay of several months in receiving a law license, an occurrence that might end up costing someone a job. Don't be one of those students that forgets about the MPRE and don't expect your law school to remind you about the MPRE either, take charge of your own affairs.

4. Save a copy of your bar exam application. Applications for the bar exam are typically 20 or more pages and require you to list virtually every place you have lived since the age of 18, as well as every speeding ticket you've received or crime you've been convicted of. You only want to have to compile this information once, so save a copy of your application, as well as any piece or scrap of paper that has anything to do with your bar exam application. You never know if yours is the application that is going to go missing at the processing office. Also, if you are planning on taking the bar exam in more than one state, save yourself some time by saving your first bar exam application, chances are that you'll need the exact same information on subsequent bar exam applications.

SIDEBAR: Your bar exam application can also prove helpful when it comes to applying for jobs, such as federal legal jobs that make you list a lot of information on the application. Your bar exam application contains valuable information that can save you a lot of time on these job applications. It is not unusual for a lawyer who has practice for years to still have a copy of his or her bar exam application in a file in his or her office. Keep a copy of your bar exam application around and keep it in a safe place.

---

5. Sign up for a bar exam review course. Signing up for a bar exam review course that takes place a few months before the bar exam is worth the money. A bar exam review course helps you by providing you with study materials and a structured study environment, as well as puts you on a study schedule that will have you well prepared before the bar exam rolls around. Many law schools enter into agreements with companies such as BAR/BRI to provide a bar exam review course for their graduating students. In fact, most law schools offer some of the best bar exam review courses because a law school's ranking and reputation can be affected by its students' bar exam pass rates.

6. Review Survival Tips For Law School Exams. Every survival tip I gave you in Part I of this book dealing with law school exams also applies to the bar exam. Reread my survival tips for law school exams and follow these same tips just as you did when taking a law school exam and you should do well on the bar exam. Remember, the bar exam is just a bigger version of most of the law school exams you have already taken and done well on.

7. Concentrate on one bar exam at a time. If you are planning to take more than one bar exam, make sure you concentrate on only one exam at a time. Do not try and study for two bar exams at one time. Concentrate on passing your first bar exam and hopefully you will find the next exam a little bit easier. It is also not a good idea to be working while you are studying for your first bar exam. All your focus needs to be on passing that first bar exam, so schedule your life accordingly.

8. Don't make a stupid mistake in law school. A state's bar exam application often requires an applicant to list every criminal offense, including speeding tickets, which he or she has been convicted of. For those of you with criminal indiscretions in your past, don't add to your list in law school with an act of stupidity such as getting a DWI after leaving a party or gathering at a local bar. For those of you who do not have a criminal past, law school is not the time to be starting your criminal career. Criminal records can severely hamper a person's ability to prove that he or she is fit to be licensed as an attorney. Don't make the hurdle that one has to clear to become a licensed attorney any higher than it needs to be with a stupid mistake.

> **SIDEBAR:** The same warning that I gave you about your criminal history also applies to your credit history. Don't give a state any reason not to license you as an attorney. Like a criminal record, a bad credit history can reflect poorly on your fitness to be licensed as an attorney. Attorneys with bad credit are often thought of as high risks to steal their clients' money, which is a deadly sin in the legal community. Watch those credit cards while you're in law school.

> **SIDEBAR:** Another stupid mistake to avoid when it comes to your bar exam application is putting down people as references that do not really know you or do not like you. The people you put down as references on your bar application will be contacted, so stop and think before you write the names of those references down on your application.

9. It's not the end of the world. It is not the end of the world if you do not pass the bar exam. You will not be the first person to not have passed the bar exam on his or her first try. If you do not pass the bar exam the first time around, review your study techniques, identify the subjects that you need to study more, and consider taking another review course. Also, check with the state giving the bar exam to determine if there is a limit on the number of times you can take the exam without having to take additional law classes.

FINDING THAT FIRST LAW JOB

The minute you set foot in law school your hunt for a job after you graduate with that coveted law degree starts. The following is a list of survival tips that can help make finding that first law job a little bit easier.

1. Do not wait to start your job search. Finding that first law job is often times hard to do. Realize that finding that first law job is going to take hard work and perseverance and start taking steps to find that job the minute you enter law school. Do not procrastinate when it comes to finding a job, it is a recipe for disaster in which a desperate law school graduate takes a job he or she hates instead of a job that is personally fulfilling.

2. Get to know the staff in the career development office. Most law schools have a career development office. Make this office a regular stop during your law school career. Get to know the office staff and tell them you want to be kept informed of the programs they are sponsoring and when employers are coming to the law school for on-campus interviews.

3. Fill that resume. If you came to law school with a fairly empty undergraduate resume, do not go through law school without taking steps to fill that resume because law school is your last chance to do so before you head out into the competitive legal jobs market. Here are some solid resume fillers that you can acquire in law school:

(A) **Clubs, societies, and organizations.** Most law schools have a large array of clubs, societies, and organizations that you can join while in law school, such as the Student Bar Association, the American Bar Association, the American Civil Liberties Union (ACLU), and the Federalist Society. Try to join at least three organizations or more, if your schedule permits, and be sure to pick organizations whose activities interest you or deal with an area of the law you are interested in.

(B) **Internships and clerkships.** Doing an internship or clerkship with a law firm, agency, or judge during the summers of your first and second years is an excellent way to gain real world legal experience and also impress future employers. Most law schools have programs to help 1L's and 2L's get judicial clerkships with state and federal judges, take advantage of these programs. Also, many law firms and agencies have on-campus interviews for internships and clerkships. Ask your career development office staff about what types of programs the law school has to help with internships and clerkships. Be advised, however, that many internships and clerkship are not paying positions but always keep an eye out for the ones that do pay. Case in point, I had a law school classmate that landed an internship that paid him over $4,000 per month, which allowed him to pay for most of his law school with his summer earnings.

(C) Teaching and research assistant. Most law schools offer students a chance to become teaching and research assistants in their second and third years. Often times these positions are not based solely on grades so don't pass on the chance to apply for an assistantship simply because you think your grades aren't good enough.

(D) Competitions. Throughout the year, your law school will hold various competitions such as moot court and negotiation competitions. Enter as many competitions as you can because a win or high finish in these competitions impresses future employers and the competitions are a great way to develop your lawyering skills. A spot on your school's moot court competition team always seems to draw the favorable attention of employers, especially federal judges looking for full-time clerks.

(E) Get something published. Most law schools have a law review journal or other journal publications that are produced by the law school. Often times, students are invited to join the staff of these publications based on their grades or the results of writing competitions sponsored by the journals. If your grades do not get you on a journal staff, try to write your way onto one. Employers like to see that a student has had something published while in law school. If you can't find your way onto a school journal, enter some of the many writing contests that are held every year by various organizations and groups. Winning one of these contests also looks good to employers, as well as improves your legal research and writing skills.

(F) Study Abroad. If your law school has a program that allows you to study law abroad consider participating in the program. Employers like to see applicants that are not afraid to expand their understanding of other cultures and these types of programs are often more affordable than one might think.

(G) Duel Degree Programs. Many law schools offer duel degree programs such as a JD/MBA course of study that allows a student to obtain a Juris Doctorate and a Masters of Business Administration. Two degrees can often times open more doors than one degree can and the law is part of virtually every aspect of American society. Students considering a duel degree program should be aware of the fact that it may take them more than 3 years to complete the program.

(H) Certificate of Emphasis. Many law schools are now allowing students to earn a certificate of emphasis in certain areas of the law, such as Business Law and Tax Law. If you are planning to practice in an area of law that your school offers a certificate of emphasis in, I highly recommend that you serious consider pursuing such a certificate.

(I) Volunteering. Volunteering your services to a local legal assistance organization never looks bad on a resume. Employers like to see that you are willing to give back to the community.

(J) Grades. Grades do matter to many employers and the higher your rank in your law school class the more job opportunities you are going to have. In fact, most entry-level legal job announcements ask applicants to list their class rank on their resumes when applying for a position. Students who finish in the top 10% of their class are often awarded the Order of the Coif and being able to put down that you are in the Order is never a minus when it comes to your resume.

> **SIDEBAR:** An ideal resume will contain what I like to call the big three: (1) Order of the Coif, (2) Published work, and (3) Moot court winner. It is rare that a law student obtains the big three but it is something to shoot for. I have provided an actual job announcement at the end of this section that illustrates the importance of having a strong resume.

4. Go to on-campus interviews. Most law schools will schedule on-campus interviews that allow employers to come to the law school and interview students for jobs, internships, and clerkships. Signup for these interviews and use them as a way to hone your interview skills. Interview for positions even if you think you don't have a chance to get them, this will improve your interview skills, get you comfortable with being interviewed, and may even get you hired despite your doubts.

SIDEBAR: Don't overlook the military when it comes to legal jobs. Most military branches, such as the Army, offer law school graduates a chance to gain valuable experience as Judge Advocates (JAG officers). If you find yourself interested in a legal career with the military, I would recommend talking to a recruiter during your first year of law school as a way of ensuring that a position is available for you after graduation. Also, do not be surprised if participating in a ROTC program while you are in law school is a prerequisite for you in securing an active duty position.

SIDEBAR: If you are looking to gain courtroom experience as quickly as possible, I suggest seeking employment with a prosecutor's office or a state's public defender system. Assistant prosecutors and assistant public defenders are never short of work and are often in the courtroom at least three or four days a week. Interning with a prosecutor's office or public defender office can help you learn what to expect with these types of jobs.

5. Do an internship or clerkship with an employer you want to work for. If you know an employer that you want to work for after law school, try to get an internship or clerkship with that employer. One of the happiest law school classmates I knew was a student who knew the employer he wanted to work for after law school, did an internship with that employer after his first and second years, and had a job waiting for him after graduation. Regardless of whether or not you know what employer you want to work for after law school, always try to chose an internship or clerkship with an employer you think you might want to work for after law school.

SIDEBAR: If you find that an employer wants to continue your internship throughout the law school year, make sure you can handle the extra work before agreeing to extend your internship and don't be afraid to ask to end your internship if the extra work proves too much for you to handle during the law school year. Full-time law students are prohibited by the American Bar Association (ABA) from working more than 20 hours per week. See: Standard 304(f). The ABA's website www.abanet.org has more information on this restriction, as well as other useful information for law students, including scholarship and writing competition opportunities. I suggest taking some time to check out the ABA's website.

6. Network. Networking with your fellow classmates can be a good way to find a job. Many times one of your classmates will know about a job opening you haven't heard about. Also, many law firms sponsor events with a law school, such as a Homecoming tailgate party, that provide students with an excellent opportunity to network with lawyers in the community. Don't hide in the law library and hope that an employer will come and find you, take advantage of these opportunities and go out and network for your future job.

7. Start putting together a wardrobe. If you do not have a large wardrobe of business dress clothes start building one now. You will need at least one good suit or outfit during your first year of law school for moot court competitions and on-campus interviews. You will also, more likely than not, be required to wear business dress attire while doing an internship or clerkship. Keep an eye out for sales on business clothes and ask for business clothes on your birthday and during the holiday seasons. The bigger the wardrobe you can build as a law student the easier your first legal job will be on your wallet when it comes to dressing for work and success.

> **SIDEBAR:** Appearance matters when you are interviewing for a job and when you are dealing with clients. Try to choose business clothes that look neat and are appropriate for the legal environment you will be working in. Also, though it may sound cruel, overweight persons face additional discrimination when it comes to finding jobs, even in the legal community. Don't let your weight get out of control in law school because it is not only bad for your health but can also be bad for your job prospects. The advice of diet and exercise is just as good for law students as it is for all people.

8. Keep your resume updated. As soon as you enter law school you need to have a resume that you can use for interviews. Attend a resume workshop sponsored by your career development office to learn what type of format your resume should be in and what is the best way to write a cover letter. Don't be surprised if you need a resume that is in more than one format because many times state and federal agencies require that an applicant's resume be in a different format than private sector employers.

> **SIDEBAR:** You may find if very useful to make electronic templates of your resume and cover letter that allow you to simply fill in the blanks when it comes to changing the names and addresses of potential employers. Backup your templates on a floppy disk or CD.

9. Websites. Most law schools have a website that lists legal job openings, as well as have agreements with other law schools to allow their students to search for jobs on the other schools' websites. Stop by your career development office and ask for a list of websites that post legal job openings. Remember the staff in the career development office is there to help you find a job and will help you find a job if you just have the courage to seek out their help. A state's bar association also typically list legal job openings on its website. Your career development office should be able to provide you with a list of state bar association websites.

10. Watch those deadlines. Many legal job listings have application deadlines, so take note of the application deadline for each job you are wanting to apply for and don't let those deadlines pass without having your applications properly submitted. When submitting applications by mail, always allow 5–7 days for delivery.

Sample Legal Job Vacancy Notice

The United States District Court
Southern District of Florida
Notice of Vacancy

Position: Law Clerk to U.S. Magistrate Judge (One position)
(Type of appointment and length of tenure to be determined)

Ann. No: 2004-JDS-07

Location: West Palm Beach, Florida

Salary Range: See Qualification Requirements Below

Open Date: June 24, 2004

Closing Date: Open Until Filled

Desired Start Date: Anticipate August/September 2004

Position Overview

Provides information, guidance and advice to U.S. Magistrate Judge in connection with pending civil and criminal litigation. Drafts appropriate recommendations and orders for the Court's signature. Reviews all complaints, petitions, motions, and pleadings that have been filed to determine issues involved and basis for relief. Performs research as required. Maintains liaison between the Court and litigants; corresponds with other court officials. Evaluates procedures. Reviews docket of pending cases where action is appropriate. Compiles statistics and prepares periodic reports, as required. Identifies problem areas, makes recommendations, and offers solutions, as required. Keeps abreast of changes in the law to aid the Judge in adjusting to new legislation. Advises appropriate personnel on status of particular cases. Performs other duties as assigned.

Qualification Requirements

Requires a Juris Doctorate and a minimum of one year of progressively responsible experience in the practice of law, in legal research, legal administration, or equivalent experience received after graduation from law school. Major or substantial legal activities while in military service may be credited, on a month-for-month basis whether before or after graduation, but not to exceed one year if before graduation. Education substitutions may apply for one year of experience. Salary matching may be available at grades JSP 12–14.

Outstanding legal research and writing skills a must. Proficient computer skills, Internet research, and WordPerfect skills are essential. Previous federal law clerk experience or private sector litigation experience is highly desired.

To qualify for level JSP Grade 11, an individual must have one year of legal work experience after graduation from law school. (Also review Educational Substitutions.) Full-time Salary $48,947.

To qualify for level JSP Grade 12, an individual must have two years of legal work experience after graduation from law school, and must be a member in good standing of the bar of a state, territory, or Federal Court of general jurisdiction. (Also review Educational Substitutions.) Full-time Salary—$58,665–$76,261.

To qualify for level JSP Grade 13, an individual must possess at least one year experience as a federal elbow law clerk in addition to the qualifications of a JSP Grade 12. Full-time Salary—$69,762–$90,692.

To qualify for level JSP Grade 14, an individual must possess at least two years experience as a federal elbow law clerk in addition to the qualifications of a JSP Grade 12. Full-time Salary $82,438–$107,170.

Educational Substitutions For Legal Work Experience

A degree from a law school of recognized standing (or the certified completion of all law studies and merely awaiting conferment of degree) is considered qualifying for Grade 9. Graduation (or the certified completion of all law school studies and requirements and merely awaiting conferment of degree) and standing within the upper third of the class from a law school on the approved list of the American Bar Association or that of the Association of American Law Schools; or experience on the editorial board of a law review of such school; or graduation from a law school on the approved list of the American Bar Association or American Law Schools with an LM degree; or demonstrated proficiency in legal studies which, in the opinion of the court is equivalent of the above, is considered qualifying for Grade 11.

The following are examples of criteria which are considered to be acceptable as equivalent:

- Publication of a noteworthy article in a law school student publication or other scholarly publication; or

- Special high-level honors of academic excellence in law school, such as election to the Order of the Coif; or

- Winning a moot court competition or membership on a moot court team that represents the law school in competition with other law schools; or

- Participation in legal aid or other law school clinical program sanctioned by the law school*, or

- Summer experience as a law clerk to a state or local judge or law clerk experience on a continuous basis (either full or part-time) in a private firm while attending school, i.e. "working the way through college".*

*In order to be applicable, participation and experience could not have been for academic credit.

Personal Characteristics

Successful candidates should be mature, responsible, poised, possess tact, good judgment, initiative, maintain a professional appearance and demeanor at all times, able to work harmoniously with others, and communicate effectively, both orally and in writing.

Benefits

Employees of the United States District Court serve under "Expected Appointment" and are considered "At-Will" employees. The following benefits are available to term Law Clerks:

- Ten paid national holidays per calendar year.

- Participation in pre-tax Federal Employees Health Insurance Program.

- Participation in a Group Life Insurance, Long Term Care and Long Term Disability Insurance.

- Participation in a pre-tax Flexible Spending Account.

- Mandatory EFT (electronic fund transfer) participation for payment of net pay.

All benefits listed above as well as the following are available to Career Law Clerks:

- Accrue 13 days of paid vacation for the first three calendar years.

- Participation in a Retirement Program with investments opportunities through the Thrift Savings Plan.

How To Apply

Submit detailed resume with exact dates of employment, salary history, copy of law school transcript, bar membership, if applicable, and legal writing sample.

Only qualified applicants will be considered for this position.

A criminal history background check will be initiated prior to job offer.

Sample Cover Letter And Resume
(Federal Format)

John Q. Law Student
1700 Poor Student Lane, Apt #3
Somewhere, Missouri 63255
(555) 555-5555 (Home)°(555) 555-5554 (Mobile)
johnq@internet.com (Email)

September 1, 2004

United States District Court
701 Clematis Street, Room 428
West Palm Beach, Florida 33401

Dear Human Resource Manager:

Recently, I heard about an employment opportunity with the United States District Court for the Southern District of Florida ("Court") with regard to a Law Clerk position and I would like to respectfully submit my resume for your consideration. I have also enclosed for your consideration a copy of my law school transcript and the requested writing sample.

As an applicant for the aforementioned position, I feel I possess the writing and research skills, as well as the legal experience necessary to make me a valuable asset to the Court. While a student at the University of Missouri-Columbia's School of Law, I was of member of the school's moot court competition team that finished first among 52 teams at the 42nd annual They Sure Do Talk A Lot Moot Court Competition sponsored by the American Bar Association ("ABA"), a competition in which I was honored as being among the top ten orators. As a law student, I earned membership in the Order of the Coif by finishing in the top 10% of my law school class. I also served on the *Missouri Law Review* editorial board, held leadership positions in the Student Bar Association and Federalist society, and had an essay, "Law Students And Learning The Art Of Negotiation," published in the ABA's *Journal of Dispute Resolution*. To gain legal experience, I served as a law clerk to Judge Big Name of the Missouri Supreme Court during the summer term of my first year in law school and completed a 3-month internship with the Office of the Missouri Public Defender in Jackson, Missouri, during the summer term of my second year. Presently, I am scheduled to be sworn in as a licensed attorney and member of the Missouri Bar on October 15, 2004, as I have obtained a passing score on Missouri's bar exam and have fulfilled all other licensing requirements.

I look forward to speaking with you about a Law Clerk position with the Court at your convenience. Thank you for your time and consideration in this matter.

Sincerely,

John Q. Law Student

Enc.

John Q. Law Student
1700 Poor Student Lane, Apt #3
Somewhere, Missouri 63255
(555) 555-5555 (Home)°(555) 555-5554 (Mobile)
johnq@internet.com (Email)

Social Security Number: 555-55-5555

Country of Citizenship: United States of America

Veteran's Preference: No

Contact Current Supervisor: Yes

VACANCY INFORMATION:

Announcement Number: 2004-JD-07

Job Title: Law Clerk

Grade(s) Applying For: Grade 11

OBJECTIVE:

Seeking a Law Clerk position with the United States District Court for the Southern District of Florida.

WORK EXPERIENCE:

Office Of The Missouri Public Defender	Dates Employed: 05/15/2003–08/15/2003
111 West Main Street	Salary: $900/month
Jackson, Missouri 63755	Hours per Week: 40–45

Legal Intern
Help prepare misdemeanor and felony cases by assisting in the researching of case law, preparing of motions and briefs to be filed with the court,

conducting of client and witness interviews, and tracking case dockets. (Supervisor's Name: Ima The Defense. Phone: (555) 555-5553).

Judge Big Name   Dates Employed: 05/15/2002–08/15/2002

Missouri Supreme Court   Salary: $1000/month

207 West High Street   Hours per Week: 40–50

Jefferson City, Missouri 65102

United States

Law Clerk
Help in the drafting of orders, rulings, and opinions authored by Judge Big Name, as well as conduct research on various legal topics when assigned to do so and create briefs and summary papers on the same. (Supervisor's Name: Judge Big Name. Phone: (555) 555-5552).

EDUCATION:

University of Missouri-Columbia School of Law
Columbia, Missouri 65211
United States
J.D., 2004
Class Rank 2/202

Southeast Missouri State University
Cape Girardeau, Missouri 63701
United States
B.S., 2000
135 Semester Hours
Major: Business
Minor: Accounting
GPA: 3.95

JOB-RELATED TRAINING COURSES:

Law Clerk Seminar—40 hours—Missouri Supreme Court—May 2002
Instruction: How to perform the duties of a Law Clerk with the Missouri Supreme Court, including legal research and writing.

Internship Seminar—40 hours—Office of the Missouri Public Defender
—May 2003
Instruction: How to perform the duties of an intern, including client
interviewing and caseload management.

JOB-RELATED SKILLS:

Criminal law experience, including the drafting of motions and briefs, the
interviewing of clients and witnesses, and the management of a large caseload.

Law clerk experience, including the drafting of orders, rulings and judg-
ments for a justice of the Missouri Supreme Court, as well as conducting
legal research.

Moot court experience, including the preparing of an appellate brief and
the successful arguing of that brief.

Law review experience, including the research and writing of an article on
negotiation that was published in a journal of the ABA.

JOB-RELATED CERTIFICATES:

Licensed To Practice Law In Missouri As Of October 15, 2004: Missouri
Bar #N/A

JOB-RELATED HONORS:

Order of the Coif
Member of the Moot Court Competition Team
Law Review Editorial Staff
Outstanding Orator—They Sure Do Talk A Lot Moot Court Competi-
tion
Student Bar Association—President, 08/2003–05/2004
Federalist Society—Vice President, 08/2002–05/2003
American Bar Association—Law Student Division

PUBLISHED WORKS:

"Law Students And Learning The Art Of Negotiation," *Journal of Dispute Resolution*, American Bar Association, April 2004, V-5, p. 235.

REFERENCES:

Honorable Big Name, Chief Justice of the Missouri Supreme Court
207 West High Street
Jefferson City, Missouri 65102
Phone: (555) 555-5551

Somebody Else Important, District Defender for District 32
111 West Main Street
Jackson, Missouri 63755
Phone: (555) 555-5553

SIDEBAR: The federal resume format is the resume format that most federal agencies require resumes to be in and also works well when applying for private sector jobs, however, I would be careful disseminating one's social security number to private employers prior to being offered a job. The example resume is provided to give you an idea of what your resume should look like but remember it is only an example and your resume should contain more detailed descriptions of your job-related training courses and job-related skills. The federal jobs website at www.usajobs.opm.gov lists legal job openings posted by federal agencies and contains a link to the federal courts' job listings.

SIDEBAR: Veterans if you are applying for a federal job, you need to make sure to check with the federal agency or entity that you are applying with or the Veterans Administration (VA) to determine if you are eligible under the current federal guidelines for a 5 or 10-point rating preference. More information about the veteran's preference can be found at the federal jobs website at www.usajobs.opm.gov or at the VA's website at www.va.gov.

KEEPING THAT FIRST REAL LAW JOB

After making it through 3 years of law school, passing the bar, and sitting through scores of interviews, most young lawyers eventually find themselves awaking one morning to the first day of their first real law job. Before you go out and save the world with your legal brilliance, take the time to read through the following list of survival tips designed to help you keep that first real law job and to make your transition from law student to working attorney an easier and more enjoyable one.

1. You don't know it all. As I told you in Part I of this book, a person doesn't go to law school to learn the law but to learn how to think like a lawyer. Consequently, there are going to be a lot, and I do mean a lot, of things you don't know about the law and the American legal system when you start your first real law job. Do not let that law degree and bar license hanging on your office wall go to your head and manifest themselves as an arrogance that prevents you from learning all you can about the law. Do not be afraid to admit that you don't know the answer to a legal question and do not be afraid of seeking out advice and guidance from a more experienced attorney.

SIDEBAR: Having a more experienced attorney acting as your mentor when you first begin practicing law can be one of the most beneficial things to happen to you in your legal career. A mentor can help you learn the law and the legal system quicker and more efficiently than you can learn it on your own, as well as help you avoid the many mistakes and pitfalls that often befall a new attorney. Also, a mentor may prove helpful to you later in your career when you are seeking a promotion or a new job, as many mentors are often times well known and well respected in their firms, agencies, and legal communities.

---

2. Develop a good professional reputation. Your first real legal job is also your first chance to begin developing your professional reputation. The same principals of honesty and hard work that helped you succeed in law school will also help you to develop a good professional reputation. Start your first legal job like you started law school, prepared to come in early and stay late. Take pride in your work and make every effort to do the very best on every memo, brief, or document that has you name attached to it. Maintain a positive attitude and be respectful of others, including not only your fellow attorneys but the office staff and your clients as well.

Remember, many a young attorney has ruined his or her professional rep-utation during their first legal job by failing to realize that sometimes a first impression is the only one a person gets to make on others.

> **SIDEBAR:** Developing a reputation for being honest and forthright with other attor-neys, your clients, and judges can go a long way in developing your overall reputa-tion as a lawyer. If people know that they can trust you and trust what you say, they know that there is a good chance they can trust you as a lawyer. Many a young law-yer has ruined his or her reputation by thinking that it was better to be sneaky and underhanded than it was to be honest and forthright.

> **SIDEBAR:** Another easy way to ruin your professional reputation is by showing up late for work and appointments on a regular basis or by not dressing appropriately for the law environment you are practicing in. Judges, lawyers, and clients do not like to be kept waiting and showing up late to court or appointments will not win you any brownie points. As for dressing appropriately, know your firm or agency's dress code and adhere to it and remember that judges expect you to show up in their courtrooms in professional dress (i.e. business suits complete with ties for the men). You won't be the first lawyer to earn the ire of a judge and be asked to leave the courtroom for not being appropriately dressed.

3. Watch out for employment contracts. Some employers ask attorneys that they are seeking to hire to sign employment contracts. Be careful when it comes to employment contracts, as most attorneys prefer to work on an at-will basis in order to keep their options open if a better employ-ment opportunity comes along or they find that they just do not enjoy the type of work they are being asked to do and want to move on quickly. Remember when you sign an employment contract that, like most con-tracts, you could face a substantial penalty if you fail to fulfill the terms of that contract, such as failing to work for your employer for a certain num-ber of years or failing to work a certain number of billable hours in a year. Be sure you know everything that is asked of you under the terms of an employment contract before you sign the contract.

SIDEBAR: A good rule of thumb is to plan on staying at your first legal job for at least two years, as two years will afford you enough time to gain a good level of legal experience, which makes you more marketable to future employers. Also, two years is a sign of stability for most employers and assures future employers that you can be hired without the worry that you will be looking for another job in six months.

4. Don't burn bridges. It is not uncommon for a lawyer to leave a job at one firm or agency only to return to that same firm or agency years later. Consequently, you need to make every effort to leave any legal job you have on good terms, as you never know if you'll be back working for the same employer again in a few years. A wise man once said, "you can never have too many friends when it comes to finding a job."

5. Keep your finances in order. Just as making a budget and sticking to it was good advice for law students so to is it good advice for new lawyers. Unless you were lucky enough to land a six figure job, your finances are more than likely going to be a little stretched during your tenure at your first real law job. Make a budget that allows you to live within your means and do not ruin your credit history by misusing credit cards or by failing to make your student loan payments on time. Declaring bankruptcy and defaulting on student loans can make it extremely difficult to find another legal job, so watch those finances.

6. Maintain your perspective. Just as you scheduled time off from law school to maintain your mental health, you should schedule time off from work to spend with your family and friends. Do not let yourself become consumed with work or let your work take the place of your family and friends. Regularly schedule time away from work and get out and enjoy life with your family and friends by taking in a ballgame, going to the park, playing in a recreational sports league, or taking a long overdue vacation. Do something besides work!

7. Keep networking. Continue networking with other attorneys and people in the legal community even after you find that first real law job. Networking will help to keep you in the information loop about what is going on in the legal community, which is especially important when it comes to learning about new employment opportunities. Don't let the contacts you developed looking for that first real law job and the contacts you have developed while working at your first real law job fade away but make an effort to keep them current, as networking is one of the most effective tools one can use in the legal job market.

> **SIDEBAR:** One of the best ways to network with fellow lawyers and legal professionals is to join the local bar association. Aside for the local bar association, many lawyers and legal professionals are active in civic organizations and joining a civic organization can not only be an excellent way to network with other lawyers and legal professionals but also be an excellent way for you to give back to your community.

8. Don't forget about those job finding survival tips. The same survival tips that helped you find your first real law job can also be helpful to you in finding that next legal job. Remember, those job finding survival tips are located only a few pages back and might be well worth your time to review if or when you decide to leave you first real law job in search of another.

9. Don't be afraid to leave the profession. If you find that after practicing law for a year or two that you don't enjoy being lawyer, do not be afraid to explore other career options. As a lawyer, you have many skills that many employers desire, so don't be afraid to seek out new career paths if you find the legal path is not the right path for you to be traveling on.

> **SIDEBAR:** Many states' bar associations offer continuing legal education (CLE) programs and presentations designed for the lawyer who is looking to explore different career options. If you find after practicing law for awhile that you are dissatisfied with the legal profession, attending a CLE program or presentation dealing with alternative career choices might prove extremely beneficial to you in deciding whether to stay in the legal profession or leave the profession and pursue other career options. Also, there are many books on the market today designed to help lawyers explore different career paths and a visit to your local bookstore or a website such as www.decisionbooks.com might also prove extremely beneficial to you.

EPILOGUE

This book is not meant to contain everything you will need to know to succeed in law school or as a new lawyer, no book could ever accomplish that feat. Remember, this book is meant to serve as a reference source and survival guide to help make your journey through law school and the transition from law student to lawyer a little easier. This is your book, don't let this be the last page in your book but take the time to add to it by writing down new survival tips whenever you hear or learn of them. Add to your book and you will be adding survival tips and information that will help you succeed in law school and the legal profession. Good luck and I'll be seeing you around the courthouses of America.

Notes:

Notes:

0-595-34838-6